L'AUBERGE DE L'ILL

MARC HAEBERLIN

L'AUBERGE DE L'ILL

65 recipes from the inn on
the banks of the river

GRUB STREET · LONDON

Contents

WHAT IF IT WERE THE ILL?
A World in Suspension ... 6

Starters ... 15

Soups ... 43

WATER MEMORY
The Ill of Memories ... 62

Sides Dishes and Vegetables ... 73

Fish ... 93

WATER ELEMENT
The Ill of Metamorphosis ... 120

Meats ... 129

WATER MOVEMENT
The Ill of the Family ... 166

Game ... 173

Desserts ... 201

Appendices ... 247

Recipe Table ... 249
Recipe Index ... 251
Addresses ... 252
Acknowledgements ... 253

WHAT IF IT WERE THE ILL?

By Paul-Henry Bizon

A World in Suspension

Some places possess a fascinating gift for happiness. Days, lunches, dinners pass there with lightness and gentleness, without even feeling like one is living them. And yet, their memory remains forever etched in us. These cherished places escape the weight of time.

Seconds flow like a river, carrying away what must go, polishing what remains. Time plays here, always adorned in subtle nuances, always new, almost imperceptible.

These are the nuances sought by the painter's brush, as much as by the chef's hand – the fickle glimmer of light on the life surrounding us.

These suspended places are islands, rare lands capable of elevating patience. Open to contemplation, they offer their most precious gift to those who inhabit them with curiosity and sincerity: the taste of time.

Marc Haeberlin's eyes are the colour of this well-kept secret. His laughter, the fleeting sound of whirlpools forming under the willows on the surface of the Ill, the placid river bathing the family inn, still reflecting the landscapes and silhouettes of his childhood.

This perpetual, elusive watercourse gives true meaning to his life as a chef – both its significance and its direction.

He speaks of his roots and his deep connection to his beloved Alsace, a land bruised by history at the crossroads of three cultures, and of his culinary heritage passed down from his father Paul and uncle Jean-Pierre – themselves heirs to a long family tradition.

He speaks of vibrant inspiration and constant transformation, of his wandering spirit and love for distant places, especially Japan, another suspended world.

He speaks of himself, his intimacy, his memories, and his questions – of how he inhabits places and of everything that makes his culinary art so subtle.

Finally, he speaks of his care for others, the importance he places on his team's growth, and on developing this family epic in the broadest sense, of which he sees himself as a humble guide.

Details of an oil painting by Roger Mühl.

L'AUBERGE DE L'ILL

Starters

Haeberlin Foie Gras Terrine

Serves 6

1 raw foie gras (800 g)
12 g seasoned salt
20 ml cognac
20 ml port
100 g goose fat

Using a small paring knife, divide the liver into two lobes. Carefully scrape away the area where the gall was attached and remove all visible blood vessels.

Season the lobes, both inside and out, with the spiced salt, then sprinkle over the port and cognac. Wrap tightly in cling film and leave to marinate in the refrigerator for 24 hours.

Arrange the liver in a terrine dish — preferably earthenware or ceramic — pressing it down firmly to eliminate any air pockets. Seal well, packing it tightly, and cover with the lid.

Place the terrine in a bain-marie and cook in a preheated oven at 90°C (th.3) for 50 minutes.

Once cooked, allow it to cool in the bain-marie. Remove the lid and cover the surface with a layer of melted goose fat.

The terrine will keep in the refrigerator for up to two weeks.

To serve, dip a spoon in hot water before cutting into the foie gras, and accompany with slices of rustic country bread or lightly toasted brioche.

Winter Lamb's Lettuce Salad and Roasted Beetroot with Alsace Horseradish Cream

Serves 4

100 g lamb's lettuce
4 medium red beetroot
1 Chioggia beetroot
Bay leaf, coarse salt, Espelette pepper

For the vinaigrette
1 shallot
50 ml olive oil
3 tbsp wine vinegar
1 pinch sugar
1 tsp mustard, salt, pepper

For the horseradish cream
120 ml double cream
1 tbsp grated horseradish
Salt, pepper

Preheat the oven to 150°C (th.5). Wash and pick over the lamb's lettuce, discarding any damaged leaves.

Wash and dry the red beetroot without peeling them. Place them in a casserole dish and cover with water. Add the bay leaf and a pinch of coarse sea salt. Cover with the lid and cook in the oven for 2 to 3 hours. When the beetroot are tender and just warm, peel away the skins. Strain the cooking liquid and reduce it gently over a low heat until slightly syrupy.

Peel the Chioggia beetroot and slice it very finely using a mandoline. Peel and finely chop the shallot.

Prepare the dressing by whisking together the olive oil, vinegar, sugar, salt, freshly ground black pepper and mustard. Stir in the reduced beetroot cooking liquor and the chopped shallot. Dress the lamb's lettuce lightly with this vinaigrette.

Cut the still-warm red beetroot into thick slices and arrange them on each plate. Place a small mound of the dressed lamb's lettuce in the centre.

Whip the well-chilled cream until softly thickened, then season with salt and pepper and fold in the horseradish. Using two spoons, shape a small quenelle of horseradish cream and place one on each plate. Garnish with one or two thin slices of raw Chioggia beetroot and finish with a light sprinkling of Espelette pepper before serving.

Right: Serge Dubs, World's Best Sommelier 1989.

Trout Fillet au Bleu on Ostergruss Radish with Lovage

Serves 6

4 trout fillets, pin-boned, skin on
4 tbsp Melfor vinegar (an Alsatian speciality)
1 litre fish stock (fumet)
2 Ostergruss radishes
1 spring onion
1 sprig lovage
Frying oil
Salt, pepper

Place the trout fillets on a deep-sided baking tray, having first brushed them lightly with Melfor vinegar. Season with salt and freshly ground black pepper, then pour over the boiling fish stock so that the fillets are well covered.

Seal the tray tightly with cling film and leave to marinate at room temperature for about 12 minutes.

Meanwhile, cut the radishes into a fine julienne and season lightly with salt. After 10 minutes, drain off the excess liquid they have released. Toss with the finely sliced spring onion and two lovage leaves, finely shredded.

Heat a little oil in a small pan and briefly fry the remaining lovage leaves until crisp. Transfer to kitchen paper to drain.

To serve, arrange the radish salad on each plate. Lay the warm trout fillets on top and serve at once, garnished with a few crisp lovage leaves.

STARTERS

Warm Goose Foie Gras with Apples and Truffle Sauce

Serves 4

4 escalopes goose foie gras (60–70 g each)
4 Reinette apples
40 g butter
500 ml white wine
4 truffle slices
Salt, pepper

For the truffle sauce
1 small truffle
60 g butter
½ glass port
1 tbsp Calvados
250 ml brown chicken stock
Salt, pepper

Peel, core and finely slice the apples. Sauté them gently in butter in a frying pan until lightly coloured. Add the white wine and continue to cook for 5 minutes, until tender. Set aside and keep warm.

Season the goose foie gras escalopes with salt and freshly ground black pepper. Heat a non-stick frying pan without adding any fat and cook the escalopes for about 3 minutes on each side, keeping them slightly pink in the centre. Remove from the pan and keep warm.

To prepare the truffle sauce, finely chop the truffle and sweat it gently in a sauté pan with a small knob of butter. Deglaze with the port, Calvados and chicken stock. Allow the liquid to reduce by half, then whisk in the remaining butter, a few small cubes at a time, to enrich and lightly thicken the sauce. Adjust the seasoning to taste.

Arrange the Reinette apples on a serving dish and place the foie gras escalopes on top. Spoon over the truffle sauce and garnish each escalope with a thin slice of truffle, lightly glazed in the cooking juices from the foie gras.

Pâté de Campagne with Four Meats

as Paul Haeberlin liked it

Serves 4

600 g puff pastry
200 g veal sweetbread
200 g foie gras
200 g pork throat (or pork jowl)
200 g chicken breast
200 g veal rump
60 ml port
30 ml cognac
1 egg + 1 yolk for glazing
30 g pistachios
15 ml truffle juice
2 truffles
15 g butter
15 g salt
200 ml beef jelly (aspic)
Coarse salt
Pepper

Lightly butter a metal pâté tin or line it with baking parchment. Roll out the puff pastry into a large rectangle, 2 mm thick. Reserve a portion for the lid and use the remainder to line the tin. Chill until required.

Blanch the sweetbreads: place them in a saucepan, cover with water and add a little coarse sea salt. Bring to the boil and simmer for about 6 minutes from boiling point, then transfer immediately to iced water to cool. Drain and trim if necessary.

Cut the foie gras into thick batons, season with salt and freshly ground black pepper, and marinate with a splash of the cognac and port.

Pass the pork through a mincer fitted with a fine plate, then incorporate the egg, mixing thoroughly. Cut the chicken breast, veal and blanched sweetbreads into 1.5 cm cubes. Combine with the minced pork, the remaining salt, port and cognac. Add the pistachios and truffle juice. Mix carefully and leave the farce to macerate in the refrigerator for 1 hour.

Cut the truffles into batons. Spread half the farce evenly into the lined tin and level the surface. Arrange the foie gras batons over the top, followed by the truffle. Cover with the remaining farce and press down firmly to compact.

Fold the pastry edges inwards. Brush with beaten egg yolk. Cover with the reserved pastry for the lid, trim the excess (keeping the trimmings for decoration), and press firmly all around to seal well. Cut three evenly spaced steam holes in the lid and keep them open with small rolls of baking parchment. Brush the lid with beaten egg and score a decorative pattern lightly with the tip of a knife. Cut decorative shapes from the pastry trimmings, attach them to the lid, and brush again with egg yolk. Refrigerate, ideally overnight.

Preheat the oven to 220°C (th.7/8). Bake for 15 minutes, then reduce the temperature to 160°C (th.5/6) and continue cooking for about 30 minutes, until the internal temperature reaches 65°C at the centre.

Allow the pâté to cool completely out of the oven, then refrigerate overnight.

Melt the beef jelly and leave to cool slightly. Pour it carefully into the pâté through one of the steam holes. Return to the refrigerator and leave for at least 4 hours, until the jelly has set.

To serve, turn out the pâté and cut into thick slices. Present with leeks in vinaigrette or a crisp celery rémoulade.

Alsatian Onion Tarte Tatin

Serves 6

6 medium onions (3 white, 3 red)
1 pinch sugar
1 pinch Espelette pepper
1 tbsp flour
160 ml milk
200 ml double cream
4 eggs + 1 yolk
30 ml olive oil
30 g butter
Salt, pepper

Shortcrust pastry
125 g soft butter
250 g flour
3 g salt
80 ml water

Prepare the shortcrust pastry by rubbing the softened butter into the flour and salt with your fingertips until the mixture resembles fine breadcrumbs. Add the water and bring together to form a smooth dough. Shape into a ball, wrap in cling film and chill in the refrigerator.

Peel and finely slice the onions. Cook them gently for at least 30 minutes in a mixture of butter and olive oil in a heavy-based saucepan, stirring regularly, until richly browned and caramelised. Season with salt, sugar and a pinch of Espelette pepper. Stir well and, towards the end of the cooking time, add the tablespoon of flour and mix thoroughly. Remove from the heat.

In a mixing bowl, whisk together the milk, double cream and the eggs (whole eggs plus the extra yolk) until smooth, then fold in the cooked onions.

Preheat the oven to 180°C (th.6). Line a buttered tart tin with the chilled pastry, then bake blind for 20 minutes using baking beans. Pour the onion custard into the pre-baked tart case. Increase the oven temperature to 200°C (th.6/7) and bake for a further 20–25 minutes, until the filling is set and beautifully golden.

Turn out while still warm and serve with a crisp lamb's lettuce salad or a lightly dressed frisée.

Blue Lobster Salad with Green Mango

Serves 4

2 blue lobsters (about 600 g each)
1 green mango, julienned
1 mint leaf
A small box of shiso leaves

Vinaigrette
1 small shallot
Juice of 1 lemon
1 tbsp white balsamic vinegar
8 tbsp lemon-infused olive oil
Salt, Espelette pepper

Cook the live lobsters in a large pan of unsalted boiling water for 6 minutes. Remove and leave until just warm, then shell them carefully and set aside.

Cut the mango in half, remove the flesh and slice it into a fine julienne. Peel and finely chop the shallot, and finely shred the mint leaf.

Prepare the vinaigrette by combining the chopped shallot with the lemon juice, salt, a pinch of Espelette pepper, white balsamic vinegar and lemon-infused olive oil.

Dress the julienned green mango with the vinaigrette and fold through the shredded mint.

To serve, arrange the green mango salad in the centre of each plate. Split the lobster tails in half lengthways, removing the dark intestinal vein, and place them on top of the salad. Spoon over the remaining vinaigrette.

Finish by adding the shelled claw meat and garnish with a few small shiso leaves.

Asparagus Feuilleté with Fresh Morels in Vin Jaune

Serves 4

1 kg white asparagus (tied into two bunches)
250 g puff pastry
1 egg for glazing
250 g fresh morels
1 shallot
50 g butter
40 ml Jura vin jaune
250 g double cream
Salt, pepper

Peel the asparagus and tie them into two bundles. Trim the stalks so that each spear measures about 10 cm from the tip. Cook in a large pan of well-salted boiling water for 10 minutes, until just tender. Drain thoroughly.

Meanwhile, prepare the puff pastry cases. Roll out the pastry to a thickness of 5 mm and cut out four rectangles, each measuring approximately 15 cm by 10 cm. Place on a baking tray lined with baking parchment and leave to rest in the refrigerator for 1 hour.

Preheat the oven to 180°C (th.6). Brush the pastry rectangles lightly with beaten egg and bake for 10 minutes, until risen and golden. Set aside.

Wash the morels carefully in several changes of water to remove all traces of sand. Peel and finely chop the shallot. Sweat the shallot gently in butter in a frying pan, then add the morels. Season with salt and freshly ground black pepper, pour in the vin jaune and cook, covered, for 10 minutes.

Lift the morels from the pan and keep warm. Add the double cream to the pan juices and simmer over a medium heat for about 6 minutes, until reduced by half. Season to taste, then return the morels to the sauce and adjust the seasoning if necessary.

Using a small knife, split open the puff pastry rectangles horizontally. Arrange six well-drained asparagus tips on the base of each. Spoon over the morel sauce and replace the pastry lids. Return to a hot oven for 1–2 minutes to heat through, and serve immediately.

Photo of the recipe on the next page

Illhaeusern-Style Fried Carp with Japanese Mayonnaise

Serves 6

1 kg carp fillets
200 g soft wheat semolina
1 unwaxed lime
250 ml milk
2 yellow lemons
Frying oil
Espelette pepper
Salt, pepper

Japanese mayonnaise
1 egg yolk
1 tbsp mustard
100 ml grapeseed oil
1 tbsp ponzu sauce
Zest of 1 unwaxed lime
2 tbsp yuzu juice
Espelette pepper, salt, pepper

Prepare the mayonnaise. In a bowl, combine the egg yolk and mustard with salt, freshly ground black pepper and a pinch Espelette pepper. Whisking continuously, gradually incorporate the oil to form a thick, glossy emulsion. Stir in the ponzu sauce, finely grated lime zest and yuzu juice. Adjust the seasoning to taste.

Grate additional lime zest into the milk and add a generous pinch of salt and pepper.

Cut the carp fillets into goujons (long, finger-sized strips) and place them in the flavoured milk. Leave to marinate in the refrigerator for 1 hour.

Remove the carp from the marinade and coat evenly in semolina.

Deep-fry the fillets in hot oil until crisp and golden. Drain well, season with salt and freshly ground black pepper, and serve immediately on a folded napkin with halved lemons and the Japanese-style mayonnaise alongside.

"Auberge de l'Ill" Sardine Tin with Oscietra Caviar

Serves 4

500 g fresh sardines
300 g potatoes
1 small leek
60 g caviar (or other fish roe)
8 tbsp olive oil
½ bunch chives
Salt, freshly ground pepper

For the marinade
200 g fine salt
100 ml lemon juice (from about 3 lemons)
2 small sprigs thyme
1 bay leaf
180 ml olive oil
Freshly ground pepper

The day before serving, rinse the sardines, rubbing them gently from tail to head, and dry thoroughly on a clean cloth. Using a small knife, lift off the fillets by making an incision at the base of the head and running the blade along the backbone on each side. Remove the fine pin bones with tweezers, dipping them into a bowl of water after each extraction. This allows the bones to fall to the bottom of the bowl and keeps the tweezers clean. Trim away the dark bloodline from the fillets.

Arrange the sardine fillets side by side in a shallow dish, skin-side down, in a single layer. Cover generously with fine salt and refrigerate for 10 minutes.

Rinse the fillets carefully, drain, and return them to the dish, this time skin-side up. Sprinkle with lemon juice and refrigerate for a further 10 minutes. Drain again, rinse and pat dry, then lay them flat once more in the dish. Scatter over the thyme leaves and the bay leaf, drizzle generously with olive oil and season with freshly ground black pepper. Cover with cling film and leave to marinate in the refrigerator for 12 hours.

Peel the potatoes and cut into small cubes. Slice the leek (both white and green parts) into similar-sized pieces. Heat the olive oil in a frying pan, add the vegetables and pour in enough water just to cover. Season with salt and pepper, cover and cook gently for 5–10 minutes, until tender. Drain if necessary.

Remove the sardines from the marinade, trim neatly and cut each fillet into three pieces. Arrange them over the warm potatoes so that the entire surface is covered. Sprinkle with finely chopped chives and add a teaspoon of caviar. Serve at once.

The sardines may be kept for up to three days in the refrigerator in their marinade, making them ideal for preparing in advance. Using tweezers to remove the pin bones is essential; dipping them in water after each removal ensures both cleanliness and precision.

Photo of the recipe overleaf

STARTERS 41

Soups

Detox Vegetable Broth

Serves 4

1 celeriac
2 organic carrots
1 cleaned leek
2 onions
5 cm ginger root
1 parsley root or a few sprigs
4 stalks lemongrass
1 bird's eye chilli
Salt

Preheat the oven to 230°C (th.7/8).

Wash all the vegetables well. Peel the celeriac, scrub the carrots (do not peel), and peel the onions and ginger. Cut the celeriac, carrots, leek and onions into large pieces.

Place all the vegetables on a baking tray lined with baking parchment and roast dry in the oven until very dark brown, about 10–15 minutes.

Transfer everything to a large pot, cover with water, add the remaining aromatics, salt, pepper and the chilli.

Simmer over a low heat for at least 2 hours. Strain and serve hot.

This broth is ideal for post-feast recovery.

Chicken Consommé with Matzo-Meal Quenelles

Serves 4

For the broth
1 cleaned and trussed hen
2 carrots
¼ celeriac
1 small leek
1 fennel
2 fresh tomatoes
2 onions
2 garlic cloves
1 bunch parsley
1 sprig lovage
1 sprig thyme
1 bay leaf
2 bird's eye chillies
250 ml dry white wine
Salt

For the quenelles
300 g goose or beef fat
80 g matzo meal
3 egg yolks
1 tsp grated fresh ginger
1 pinch Espelette pepper
2 tbsp chopped parsley
2 tbsp chopped chives
1 pinch grated nutmeg
Salt, pepper

Peel the vegetables and wash them thoroughly. Cut them into large, rough chunks. Peel one onion and the garlic cloves. Halve the unpeeled second onion and char it on a baking tray.

Wash and dry the parsley.

In a large pot, place the whole chicken, all the vegetables and the herbs. Season with salt, add the white wine, cover with water and simmer gently for 3–4 hours. Skim after 10 minutes.

Once done, degrease using kitchen paper or a skimmer, then strain through a fine sieve and clean cloth.

Makes broth for 8; can be refrigerated or frozen.

For the quenelles, Melt the fat and mix all the ingredients in a food processor until smooth. Cover and chill for 2 hours.

Form small dumplings (about 15 g) and simmer in chicken broth for 15 minutes.

Serve the quenelles in bowls with hot broth poured over.

Above: Patrick Zuccolin and Frédéric Schaetzel
(Master of Port 2023).
Opposite: Anne-Catherine Delorme.

Leek and Potato Velouté with White Truffle from Piedmont

Serves 4

3 medium leeks
3 medium Charlotte potatoes
1 litre water
250 ml cream
1 pinch Espelette pepper
30 g butter
1 small white truffle (20 g)
Salt, pepper

Wash and finely slice the white parts of the leeks. Peel the potatoes, cutting two of them into large chunks and the third into small, even cubes.

In a large saucepan, sweat the sliced leeks gently in butter until soft but without colouring. Pour in 1 litre of water and bring to the boil. Add the roughly chopped potatoes, season with salt, freshly ground black pepper and a pinch of Espelette pepper, then cook over a medium heat for 20 minutes, until tender. Stir in the double cream, blend until perfectly smooth in a blender, and keep the velouté hot.

Cut one green part of a leek into small cubes to match the diced potato. Cook both together in well-salted boiling water for about 8 minutes, then drain thoroughly.

Place a tablespoon of the diced potato and leek in the base of each warmed soup plate, then ladle over the hot velouté. Shave the white truffle into very fine slices directly over the plates at the table, and serve immediately.

This velouté may also be enriched with a poached egg, if desired.

Watercress Velouté with Poached Egg

Serves 4

200 g spinach
1 celeriac
4 onions
2 leeks
4 bunches watercress
150 ml white wine
2 litres white stock
150 g short-grain rice
1 litre cream
4 fresh eggs
3 tbsp white vinegar
Salt, pepper

Blanch the spinach in well-salted boiling water for 2–3 minutes. Refresh immediately in iced water, then spread the leaves out on a clean cloth and press gently to remove all excess moisture.

Peel the celeriac and onions, and wash the leeks thoroughly. Cut all the vegetables into a mirepoix.

In a large saucepan, sweat half of the vegetables gently in olive oil without allowing them to colour. Add the spinach and watercress, stir well, deglaze with white wine and allow it to reduce. Pour in enough white stock to cover and simmer for 30 minutes. Strain to obtain a clear, flavourful broth.

In the same saucepan, repeat the process with the remaining vegetables, again sweating them without colour. Moisten with the strained stock from the first cooking. Add a little short-grain rice to thicken and cook for a further 25 minutes.

Stir in the cream, then blend until perfectly smooth. Pass through a fine chinois and adjust the seasoning.

Poach the eggs in gently simmering, unsalted water with a splash of white wine vinegar for about 3 minutes. Drain carefully on a clean cloth.

Place one poached egg in each warmed plate and spoon the emulsified watercress velouté around it. Serve immediately.

Crayfish Broth with Aromatics

Serves 4

- 1 kg live crayfish (preferably red-legged)
- 250 g celeriac
- 2 large carrots
- 2 leeks
- 4 ripe tomatoes
- 1 garlic clove
- 1 sprig thyme
- 1 bay leaf
- 1 slice fresh peeled ginger
- 1 tbsp chopped herbs (chives, chervil, parsley, etc.)
- 200 ml dry white wine
- 1 litre chicken stock
- 4 tbsp olive oil
- 50 g butter
- 1 pinch Espelette pepper
- Salt, whole peppercorns

No need to harm the crayfish by gutting: simply blanch them in boiling salted water for 2 minutes, drain and let cool. Shell the crayfish, reserving the heads and shells.

Peel, wash and dice the vegetables; peel the garlic.

Heat the olive oil in a large pan, add the crayfish heads and shells and sauté over a high heat for 2 minutes. Add the carrots, ¼ celeriac, ½ leek, tomatoes, garlic, ginger, chilli, thyme and bay. Stir for 2 more minutes.

Pour in the wine and deglaze. When reduced, add the chicken stock. Lower the heat and simmer for 25 minutes.

Strain the broth through a fine sieve and set aside.

In another pan, melt the butter and gently cook the remaining vegetables for 10 minutes. Add the crayfish tails and the hot broth. Warm through.

Add the fresh herbs, stir and serve in warm bowls.

This broth can be made with any shellfish.

WATER MEMORY

The Ill of Memories

The road into Illhaeusern is straight, but the entrance to this dreamscape is narrow; you must adopt the right posture to grasp its uniqueness.

On one side lies Alsace with its castles, hills and vineyards — Kaysersberg, Riquewihr, Ribeauvillé. On the other stands the Alsatian plain, industrious and rural.

Between them runs a subtle frontier, both geographic and emotional, shaped by the river Ill — a shifting, capricious thread of water, sometimes hidden in ditches, rising and vanishing with the seasons. Its clear, living water rises in the foothills of the Jura, then winds from Mulhouse to Strasbourg before merging with the Rhine.

Water carries, transports and guides. Water, as we know, lends itself to stories.

The story of L'Auberge de l'Ill begins with rustic simplicity: matelotes, freshwater fish stews for passing fishermen and boatmen.

Since 1882 in Illhaeusern, where the Ill and Fecht meet, diners chose between the "Catholic" matelote at À la Truite, or the "Protestant" Riesling matelote (still served every Good Friday) at the Haeberlin family's tavern across the river: L'Arbre Vert.

Right: the zimmerla, a small family room adjacent to the kitchen.

Above: portrait of Paul Haeberlin.

In Alsace, where everything is borderland, nothing is walled in. Cultures, languages and religions layer and mingle, vanish and reappear — like water and its hidden tributaries. The first family inn was destroyed in the Second World War, but rebuilt in 1950 under the drive of Marthe and Frédéric "Fritz" Haeberlin's sons, Paul and Jean-Pierre, who grew up in their mother and Aunt Henriette's joyful kitchen.

Paul quickly proved a gifted chef, honing his instinctive cooking at Hôtel de la Pépinière under Edouard Weber, former chef to the Tsars, Greek royalty and the Rothschilds. Jean-Pierre, passionate about painting and decorative arts, became the radiant host and public ambassador. Together, they elevated L'Auberge de l'Ill to culinary prominence, earning one Michelin star in 1952, a second in 1957 and a third ten years later.

Very close to both his uncle and his father, with whom he worked extensively from 1976 onwards, Marc Haeberlin has never turned his back on the flavours of this riverside and game-based cuisine – so deeply French in its way of combining plating techniques with sauces, a cuisine rich in butter and cream, smooth and velvety, which he has simply refined to suit contemporary tastes.

It is with a mixture of curiosity and excitement that one sinks a fork into the salmon soufflé "Auberge de l'Ill" or the frog mousseline "Paul Haeberlin", dishes that melt on the tongue and reveal the flavours of a happy childhood. One delights in fried carp, four-meat pâté de campagne, Romanov partridge or the zander fillet "Aunt Henriette" with wild garlic, feeling privileged to partake in the generous pleasures of a period one never actually lived through.

SOUPS 69

Side Dishes and Vegetables

Carrots in Kadaif

Serves 4

- 4 large carrots
- 1 egg
- 4 tbsp flour
- 1 pack kadaif pastry (about 500 g)
- Frying oil
- Espelette pepper
- Salt, pepper

For the aromatic garnish
- 1 garlic clove
- 4 tbsp olive oil
- ¼ preserved (salt-cured) lemon
- 1 pinch mild curry powder
- 1 slice orange
- 2 cardamom pods
- 1 slice fresh ginger
- 1 pinch saffron
- Juice of 1 orange
- Salt

Peel the carrots and the garlic. Place the 4 carrots in a sauté pan and cover with water. Add salt, olive oil, the aromatic garnish and orange juice.

Cover and simmer gently for at least 30–35 minutes, until the carrots are tender (test with a knife). Leave to cool in the broth.

Beat the egg in a shallow dish. Once cooled, lightly flour the carrots, dip them in the egg and roll them in the kadaif pastry.

Wrap each carrot tightly in cling film and refrigerate for at least 20 minutes.

Heat oil in a deep-fryer to 180°C. Unwrap and fry the carrots for 5–6 minutes until golden.

Drain on kitchen paper, sprinkle with Espelette pepper and serve immediately.

Ceps from the Vosges Roasted in Fig Leaves

Serves 4

1 kg fresh, firm ceps (porcini)
8 large fig leaves
3 garlic cloves
4 tbsp olive oil
30 g butter
Salt, pepper

Wipe the ceps clean and dry thoroughly. Wash and pat dry the fig leaves.

Preheat the oven to 220°C (th.7/8).

Cut the ceps into large pieces, about 2–3 cm across. Heat a frying pan and sauté them briskly in olive oil and butter. Season with salt and freshly ground black pepper, then add the three unpeeled garlic cloves. Cook over a high heat for 2–3 minutes, allowing the mushrooms to colour lightly.

Line the base of an ovenproof dish with half of the fig leaves. Spoon over the sautéed ceps and garlic, then cover with the remaining fig leaves. Bake for 13 minutes.

Serve immediately, bringing the dish straight to the table and uncovering it in front of your guests. The fragrant steam released by the fig leaves will delicately perfume the ceps and heighten the experience of the dish.

"During the lockdown, I amused myself by illustrating the meals we shared with Isabelle and the occasional visiting friend – a way of preserving good memories."

Little Cabbage Parcels Stuffed with Truffle

Serves 4

4 truffles (50 g each)
20 ml port
1 savoy cabbage (4 large leaves)
1 carrot
100 g celeriac
250 ml veal stock
60 g butter
Salt, pepper

For the stuffing
100 g pork shoulder
100 g chicken breast
50 g foie gras
1 egg
1 tbsp port
1 tsp cognac
Salt, pepper

Peel the truffles with a vegetable peeler, reserving the peelings. Place the truffles in a small saucepan with a glass of water and the port. Cover and cook gently for 20 minutes, then chill in their cooking liquor.

For the stuffing, pass the meats through a mincer. Season with salt and freshly ground black pepper, then add the egg, cognac and port. Mix thoroughly until evenly combined and refrigerate.

Strip the leaves from the Savoy cabbage and blanch them in well-salted boiling water for 2–3 minutes. Refresh immediately in iced water, then lay out on a clean cloth and pat dry. Peel the carrot and celeriac and cut into a fine brunoise.

Preheat the oven to 200°C (th.6/7). Shape four small stuffed cabbages: place a portion of stuffing in the centre of each cabbage leaf, add a piece of the poached truffle, then fold and press firmly in the palm of your hand to seal tightly.

In a small casserole, melt 30 g of butter and gently sweat the diced carrot and celeriac. Add the chopped truffle peelings, pour in the veal stock, then arrange the four stuffed cabbages in the casserole. Cover and bake for 15 minutes.

Once cooked, remove the cabbages and keep warm. If necessary, reduce the cooking liquor slightly, adjust the seasoning, then whisk in the remaining 30 g of cold butter to enrich and glaze the sauce.

Arrange the stuffed cabbages on warm plates and spoon over the sauce before serving.

Spelt Risotto with Ceps

Serves 4

250 g spelt
1 onion
1 bunch flat-leaf parsley
1 glass dry white wine
2 litres white poultry stock
500 g fresh ceps
1 garlic clove
100 ml double cream
80 g grated Parmesan
60 g cold butter
100 ml olive oil
Espelette pepper
Salt, pepper

Peel and finely chop the onion. Wash, dry and finely chop the parsley.

Heat the olive oil in a cast-iron casserole and sauté the spelt until lightly coloured. Add the chopped onion, deglaze with the white wine and add the white stock. Season with salt and Espelette pepper.

Cover the casserole and cook over a low heat for at least 2 hours. Check the cooking, allow any excess liquid to reduce, and set aside.

Clean the ceps and cut them into small cubes. Sauté in olive oil with the unpeeled garlic clove. Season with salt and freshly ground black pepper. Allow them to colour lightly, then remove the garlic once cooked.

Whip the well-chilled cream using a mixer or a whisk.

To the cooked spelt, add the Parmesan, chopped parsley, the cold butter cut into pieces, a drizzle of olive oil and the whipped double cream. Mix thoroughly.

Spoon the risotto into a deep plate, arrange the sautéed ceps over the top and finish with a few sprigs of parsley.

SIDE DISHES AND VEGETABLES 83

Green Bean Salad with Poached Egg and Foie Gras

Serves 4

700 g fresh green beans
12 white mushrooms
1 bunch chives
4 extra-fresh eggs
3 tbsp white vinegar
4 raw foie gras escalopes (duck or goose)
Salt, pepper

For the vinaigrette
1 shallot
3 tbsp balsamic vinegar
1 tbsp wine vinegar
4 tbsp olive oil
Salt, pepper

Wash and trim the green beans. Boil in salted water for about 4 minutes until just tender yet still firm and crisp. Drain and refresh in iced water. Drain again and dry.

Peel and finely chop the shallot. In a bowl, whisk the vinegar and olive oil, add salt, pepper and the shallot.

Slice the mushrooms thinly and mix with the green beans and vinaigrette. Chop the chives.

Poach the eggs in barely simmering, vinegar-acidulated water for about 3 minutes. Drain on a cloth and season with pepper.

In a non-stick pan, cook the seasoned foie gras slices for about 3 minutes per side until nicely browned.

Plate the salad, top with a poached egg and a slice of seared foie gras. Sprinkle with chopped chives.

Wood-Roasted Aubergines with Natural Vinaigrette

Serves 4

- 4 large aubergines
- 1 unwaxed lemon
- 8 tbsp extra-virgin olive oil
- 4 basil leaves
- 1 small bunch chives
- Salt, Espelette pepper

Preheat the barbecue (or the Big Green Egg®). Once thoroughly hot, grill the aubergines for 10 minutes on each side, charring them well all over.

Transfer to an oven preheated to 200°C (th.6/7) and continue cooking for a further 30 minutes. Check doneness with the tip of a small knife. Leave to cool for 30 minutes.

When the aubergines are warm, remove the burnt skin. Arrange them on the serving dish. Finely grate the lemon zest over the top using a Microplane®. Season lightly with salt and Espelette pepper, then drizzle with the lemon juice and olive oil. Leave to marinate for about 30 minutes, or longer if desired, but do not refrigerate.

Just before serving, finish with chopped basil and snipped chives.

If you do not have a barbecue, the aubergines may be charred using a blowtorch or directly over a gas flame.

Ratte Potatoes Cooked in Hay

Serves 4

16 Ratte potatoes
A good handful of hay
3 garlic cloves
40 g butter
40 ml olive oil
Salt, pepper

Preheat the oven to 220°C (th.7/8). Wash but do not peel the potatoes.

In a cast-iron pot, lay half the hay, add the seasoned potatoes, the garlic (unpeeled), the butter in pieces and drizzle with olive oil.

Cover with the remaining hay, pour in half a glass of water, cover, and bake for 25 minutes.

Uncover and bake for another 10 minutes to lightly burn the hay, giving the potatoes a smoky flavour.

These potatoes pair perfectly with white or red meats or cheeses such as Vacherin Mont d'Or, Munster or seasoned fromage blanc.

Red Cabbage Confit with Figs

Serves 4

1 red cabbage (800 g)
1 pinch sugar
3 tbsp red wine vinegar
200 g onions
8 dried figs
250 ml red wine
250 ml port
3 cm fresh ginger root
100 ml olive oil
Salt, pepper

The day before, quarter the cabbage and remove the core. Finely slice each quarter.

Mix the cabbage with sugar, vinegar and salt. Leave to marinate overnight at room temperature.

Next day, preheat the oven to 150°C (th.5). Peel and slice the onions. Dice the figs. Drain the cabbage and reserve the marinade.

Heat the oil in a cast-iron pot, brown the onions, add the cabbage and figs, pour in the reserved marinade, red wine and port. Add the peeled ginger.

Cover and braise in the oven for 1 hour 30 minutes, until very tender.

Before serving, mix well and adjust seasoning.

Fish

Mackerel in White Wine with Japanese-Style Daikon

Recipe by Taichi Nakahiro, chef of the three Auberge de l'Ill restaurants in Japan

Serves 4

2 large mackerel, filleted
1 daikon radish
4 tbsp ponzu sauce
2 tbsp soy sauce
4 shiso leaves

For the broth

250 ml dry white wine
2 tbsp Melfor vinegar (an Alsatian speciality)
1 unwaxed lemon
1 bay leaf
1 sprig thyme
1 pinch Espelette pepper
Salt, pepper

Cut the mackerel fillets in half and remove the bones.

In a large saucepan, prepare a broth with the white wine, vinegar, aromatics, one slice of lemon with the peel, and some salt. Add 250 ml water and boil for 15 to 20 minutes.

Place the mackerel fillets into the aromatic broth, heat briefly, then leave to cool and refrigerate for 2 to 3 hours.

Meanwhile, peel and cut the daikon into 8 thick slices, then cook them for about 15 minutes in a covered pot with a broth made from ponzu sauce, soy sauce and water. Check doneness with the tip of a paring knife, then chill.

In a deep plate, arrange 2 slices of daikon, each topped with a piece of mackerel. Spoon a little of the daikon cooking liquid over the top and finish with finely shredded shiso leaves added at the last moment.

Frog Mousseline Paul Haeberlin

Serves 8

1.5 kg frogs' legs
500 g spinach
1 garlic clove
100 g tomato concassé
½ bunch chives
A few sprigs chervil
75 g butter
Salt, pepper

For the stuffing

500 g pike-perch flesh
20 g salt
4 eggs
650 ml full-fat double cream, very cold
Pepper
Nutmeg

For the Riesling sauce

Frog bones
4 shallots
½ bottle Riesling
250 ml fish stock
50 g roux
250 ml double cream
75 g butter
Juice of ½ lemon
Salt, pepper

Prepare the stuffing. Pass the pike-perch flesh through a mincer fitted with the fine plate, then place it in a food processor. Add the salt, pepper and a little freshly grated nutmeg, and blend for 5 seconds. Add the eggs, blend again, and gradually incorporate 500 ml of very cold double cream. Transfer the stuffing to a bowl.

Whip 150 ml very cold double cream and gently fold it into the stuffing using a spatula. Place the mixture into a piping bag and refrigerate for 30 minutes.

Butter eight ramekins measuring 8 cm in diameter and 4 cm in height, and keep them chilled. Bone the raw frogs' legs. Peel and finely chop the shallots. Finely chop the chives.

In a pan, sweat the chopped shallots in butter, add the frog bones and deglaze with the Riesling. Add the fish stock and simmer for 15 minutes. Strain the cooking liquid through a chinois and reduce over a low heat by half, about 15 minutes. Thicken with a little roux, add the double cream, and finish the sauce by whisking in 50 g very cold butter cut into small cubes. Add a little lemon juice and a touch of Riesling, and adjust the seasoning.

Preheat the oven to 200°C (th. 6/7). Season the frogs' legs with salt and pepper and poach them in a little of the gently simmering sauce for 2 minutes.

Using the piping bag, cover the bottom and sides of the ramekins with the fish mousse. With the back of a spoon, create a slight hollow in the centre. Add the cooked frogs' legs, a little of the chives and 1 tablespoon of sauce. Using a spatula, cover the mousse with more fish stuffing. Place the ramekins in a bain-marie and bake for 6 to 8 minutes. Remove from the oven and leave to rest for 5 minutes.

Peel and chop the garlic. Wash the spinach and wilt it in a sauté pan with butter and the garlic. Season with salt and pepper. Drain and keep warm.

Unmould the mousselines onto a dish or deep plate garnished with the spinach. Sprinkle with chopped chives, coat with the Riesling sauce, and decorate with a small spoonful of tomato concassé and some chervil.

Illhaeusern Matelote with Riesling

Serves 6 to 8

1 eel (1 kg)
500 g pike
1 perch (200 g)
1 tench (300 g)
2 trout (400 g each)
4 shallots
125 g butter
1 bottle Riesling
200 g fresh button mushrooms
80 g flour
250 ml double cream
A dash of lemon juice
A pinch of nutmeg
1 tbsp chopped parsley
Salt, pepper

For the court-bouillon
1 leek
1 carrot
1 onion
¼ bay leaf
1 sprig thyme
1 sprig tarragon
½ garlic clove

Skin the eel and scale the fish, then gut and wash them. Remove the fins, then cut the fish into pieces.

To prepare the court-bouillon, wash, peel and cut the vegetables into pieces. Place them in a large pot and add 1.5 litres water. Add the fish heads, thyme, bay leaf, tarragon and peeled garlic. Boil for 30 minutes, strain through a chinois and set aside.

Peel and chop the shallots. In a saucepan, melt the butter and sweat the shallots. Moisten with the bottle of Riesling and 1 litre court-bouillon. Season with salt and pepper and bring to the boil.

Add the eel pieces first, as they require the longest cooking time. Cook for 5 minutes, then add, in order: the pike, the tench, then the perch and trout. Season again with salt and pepper and simmer for 15 minutes over a medium heat.

Slice the mushrooms and sauté them in butter. While the fish is cooking, prepare a roux with 50 g butter and 80 g flour. Cook the roux for 5 minutes, then leave it to cool.

Remove the fish from the liquid and arrange it on a serving dish; keep warm.

Pour the fish cooking liquid onto the roux while whisking. Bring to the boil, add the cream and simmer for about 10 minutes. Incorporate the remaining butter, a dash of lemon juice, a hint of nutmeg and adjust the seasoning.

Blend briefly to emulsify, then coat the fish with this sauce. Garnish with chopped parsley and serve with fresh noodles.

"Illustration of a grilled sole on the Big Green Egg, reinterpreted in the style of César's compressions."

MH
hommage à Cèsar
compression de soles grillées

Roast Eel in Hay

Serves 4

1 eel, 1.2 kg, gutted, headed, trimmed and scaled
1 large handful very dry hay
1 small shallot
500 ml water
1 sprig fresh thyme
1 bunch chervil
1 small bunch parsley
125 g butter
Salt, pepper
Espelette pepper

Preheat the oven to 210°C (th. 7).

Cut the eel into pieces 6 to 7 cm long. Season with salt and pepper.

In an ovenproof dish, spread out the handful of hay, place the eel pieces on top and bake for 20 minutes.

Meanwhile, peel and finely chop the shallot. Boil the water with all the herbs (stems removed) for 5 minutes.

Pour everything into a blender, mix with the cold butter and Espelette pepper, and serve the sauce in a sauceboat alongside the hay-roasted eel pieces.

Zander Fillet à la Tante Henriette

Serves 4

4 zander fillets (150 g each), skin on
2 shallots
200 ml chicken stock
200 ml Riesling
250 g thick crème fraîche
Juice of ½ lemon
A few sprigs chervil
Butter
Salt, pepper

For the stuffing
100 g onions
50 g parsley
50 g butter
60 g fresh breadcrumbs

Prepare the stuffing: peel and chop the onions, chop the parsley.

Soften the butter and add the raw chopped onions, chopped parsley and the breadcrumbs.

Preheat the oven to 210°C (th. 7). Peel and chop the shallots.

Butter an ovenproof dish and sprinkle it with the chopped shallots.

Place the zander fillets in the dish, season with salt and pepper, and cover them with the stuffing.

Moisten with the stock and the Riesling, then bake for 8 minutes, basting frequently until lightly browned.

Transfer the fish to a serving platter. Deglaze the baking dish with the thick crème fraîche, strain through a chinois into a saucepan and reheat without boiling. Adjust the seasoning, add a dash of lemon juice and the chopped chervil, then pour the hot sauce around the fillets.

"An homage to the Troisgros family and their famous salmon with sorrel, and a double tribute to Pierre Alechinsky and my friend Raymond Waydelich, with whom I exchanged drawings daily during the lockdown."

Auberge de l'Ill Salmon Soufflé

Serves 8

1 kg salmon fillet, skinless
4 shallots
½ bottle Riesling
250 ml fish stock
8 puff pastry fleurons
250 g drained tomato concassé
50 g butter
Salt

For the stuffing
250 g zander flesh
10 g fine salt
2 eggs
350 ml very cold double cream
Nutmeg
Pepper

For the sauce
250 ml double cream
150 g very cold butter
Juice of ½ lemon

Prepare the stuffing. Pass the zander flesh through a mincer fitted with the fine plate, then place it in a food processor. Add the salt, pepper and a little freshly grated nutmeg, and blend for 5 seconds. Add the eggs, blend again, and gradually incorporate 250 ml very cold double cream.

Transfer the stuffing to a bowl. Whip 100 ml very cold double cream and gently fold it into the stuffing with a spatula. Refrigerate for 1 hour.

Preheat the oven to 200°C (th. 6/7). Cut the salmon fillet into 8 equal portions of about 120 g each. Peel and chop the shallots.

Cover each salmon portion with the stuffing, shaping it into a dome.

Place the salmon portions in a buttered dish seasoned with salt and sprinkled with the chopped shallots. Moisten with the Riesling and the fish stock, then bake for 7 minutes. Transfer the salmon to a serving platter and keep warm.

Pour the cooking liquid into a sauté pan, add the double cream and reduce over a low heat for about 10 minutes. Finish the sauce by whisking in the very cold butter cut into small pieces. Add the lemon juice.

Adjust the seasoning and pour the sauce around the salmon.

Garnish with puff pastry fleurons and small quenelles of tomato concassé.

FISH 111

Shellfish Broth with Seaweed and Scallops

Serves 4

24 bouchot mussels (sorted and cleaned)
600 g clams
16 large scallops
1 shallot
1 garlic clove
1 sprig thyme
1 lemon slice
1 bay leaf
120 ml dry white wine
500 ml fish stock
4 tbsp dried seaweed "fisherman's mix"
(dulse, sea lettuce and nori)
80 g butter
40 ml olive oil
Espelette pepper

Peel and finely chop the shallot. Peel the garlic clove.

In a large pot, sweat the mussels and clams with the chopped shallot, thyme, garlic, bay leaf and the lemon slice. Moisten with the white wine and the fish stock.

Bring to the boil and cook, covered, until the shellfish open, 1 to 2 minutes.

Drain, clean and shell the shellfish. Reduce the cooking liquid if needed. Whisk in the cold butter, then incorporate the dried seaweed and set aside.

Meanwhile, sear the scallops in a non-stick pan with a little olive oil, browning them for 1 minute on each side.

Arrange the scallops in a deep plate, surround them with the cooked shellfish, and ladle the seaweed broth over the top.

Sprinkle with Espelette pepper.

Sole with Crayfish

Serves 4

2 soles (800 g each)
24 crayfish
2 litres court-bouillon
4 shallots
25 ml Riesling
250 ml fish stock
250 ml double cream
10 g butter
60 g crayfish butter
A dash of cognac
Salt, pepper

For the stuffing
150 g whiting fillets
1 egg white
200 ml very cold double cream
20 g chopped truffle
Salt, pepper

Fillet the soles (or have the fishmonger do it).

Cook the crayfish in a court-bouillon and shell them. Reserve 8 large heads.

For the stuffing: blend the whiting fillets, egg white, salt and pepper while slowly adding the very cold cream. Transfer the resulting stuffing to a bowl and add the chopped truffle.

Preheat the oven to 210°C (th. 7). Peel and chop the shallots.

Dry the sole fillets and flatten them lightly. Using a piping bag with a round tip, fill the soles with the stuffing and fold them over. Stuff the crayfish heads as well and place them at the ends of the soles, inserting them firmly.

Place the stuffed soles in a buttered baking dish. Sprinkle with the chopped shallots, season with salt and pepper. Moisten with the Riesling and the fish stock. Cover with aluminium foil and bake for 10 minutes.

Transfer the soles to a serving dish and keep warm.

Pour the cooking juices into a sauté pan with the cream and reduce by half over a low heat, about 20 minutes.

Sauté the crayfish tails in a small amount of crayfish butter. Deglaze with a splash of cognac. Emulsify the sauce with crayfish butter. Adjust the seasoning and coat the sole fillets with the sauce. Arrange the crayfish tails around them.

Poached Thick-Cut Turbot with Hollandaise Sauce and Potatoes

Serves 4

1 turbot (3.5 to 4 kg)
1 onion
3 cloves
2 bay leaves
2 bird's eye chillies
2 unwaxed lemons
500 ml milk
8 egg yolks
400 g butter
1 pinch Espelette pepper
32 Charlotte potatoes (turned or evenly sized)
Salt, pepper

Cut the turbot into 8 thick sections, keeping the central bone and the skin after gutting it. Prepare a large pot with water, salt, the peeled onion studded with cloves, 1 bay leaf, the small chillies, 1 lemon cut into slices, and the milk. Bring everything to the boil and simmer for 10 minutes, then immerse the turbot pieces and cook without boiling for about 15 minutes. Turn off the heat and keep the fish in its broth.

Meanwhile, in a sauté pan over a low heat, whisk the 8 egg yolks with 8 tablespoons of water until a firm, voluminous foam forms.

Clarify the butter: melt it, skim the foam from the surface, and pour it gently into a container, leaving the milk solids at the bottom of the saucepan. Leave the clarified butter to cool slightly.

Add salt, pepper and Espelette pepper to the egg yolks, then gradually incorporate the clarified butter. Add half the juice of the second lemon, adjust the seasoning, and serve the Hollandaise separately in a sauceboat.

Cook the potatoes in salted boiling water with 1 bay leaf for about 20 minutes. Check doneness with the tip of a knife, drain and coat lightly with butter. Serve separately.

Arrange the well-drained turbot sections on a serving platter after removing the black skin. Serve with the potatoes and the Hollandaise sauce.

Ragout of Lobster and Calf's Head with Pearl Barley

Serves 4

5 lobsters (500 g each)
½ boned and rolled calf's head
2 carrots
½ celeriac
1 leek
1 large onion
30 g fresh ginger root
2 garlic cloves
1 tsp Sichuan pepper
1 bird's eye chilli
2 sprigs parsley
1 sprig thyme
1 bay leaf
1 tbsp tomato purée
250 ml full-bodied red wine
125 ml port
600 ml dark veal stock
100 g pearl barley
80 g cold butter
3 tbsp olive oil
Salt, pepper

Peel all the vegetables. Cut 1 carrot, half the celeriac and the white of the leek into a brunoise (very small 1 mm dice). Cut the remaining vegetables along with the green part of the leek and the onion into a mirepoix (small dice). Peel the ginger and cut it into small cubes; peel the garlic and crush the cloves.

Bring a large pot of water to the boil. Salt it, then plunge in the lobsters and cook them for 5 minutes. Drain and cool them under cold water. Shell the tails and claws. Cut the tails into medallions. Open the lobster heads, remove the sand sac and scrape the gills. Split the heads in half.

Heat the olive oil in a large pot. Sear the lobster shells over a high heat. Add the aromatic garnish cut in mirepoix, the Sichuan pepper, chilli, garlic, parsley, thyme, bay leaf, ginger and tomato purée. Moisten with the red wine, port and dark veal stock. Stir and reduce by half over a low heat, about 10 minutes.

Add the half calf's head, add water as needed to cover, and cook over a low heat for 2 to 2½ hours, until the head is tender.

Drain the head and refrigerate it. Strain the cooking liquid and reduce it further to intensify the flavour.

In a pot of boiling salted water, cook the pearl barley for 20 minutes. Cool immediately once cooked.

Blanch the vegetable brunoise in boiling salted water for 1 to 2 minutes, cool in iced water, and drain at once.

Cut the chilled calf's head into 1 cm cubes.

Reheat the cooking liquid and incorporate the cold butter, whisking. Add the vegetable brunoise, the calf's head cubes and the pearl barley.

Reheat the lobster for 2 minutes in a steam oven or steamer.

Arrange the lobster medallions in deep plates, bowls or cups. Ladle the broth and garnish over them, and finish with the lobster claws.

WATER ELEMENT

The Ill of Metamorphoses

Having inhabited this aquatic "in-between" since his earliest youth, Marc Haeberlin is also a bridge between eras. A perfect synthesis of the culinary giants who shaped his taste and talent, he stands —alongside Michel Troisgros, Régis Marcon and Guy Savoy — as one of the emblematic representatives of a golden generation of contemporary French gastronomy that evolved towards greater lightness and surprise. Deeply rooted in his native territory yet possessed of a traveller's spirit, Haeberlin came of age in the early 1970s during his apprenticeship at the Strasbourg hotel school, at a time when the world was opening up and distances were shrinking. It was an era of departures and new encounters.

Mentored by Jean and Pierre Troisgros, then by Paul Bocuse — whose mastery, work ethic and rebellious spirit he equally admired — Marc Haeberlin refined the elegance of his technique through close contact with these masters of French and European cuisine (including Helmut Gietz of the Erbprinz restaurant in Ettlingen). His inspiration was also illuminated by exposure to other culinary cultures during his numerous travels to the United States, around the Mediterranean and in Asia.

This openness is evident in the vibrant use of spices in his superb lacquered wild duck, the veal shank inspired by a return from Marrakech, or in carrots wrapped in kadaïf; in the luxuriant simplicity and depth of flavour of a tin of sardines crowned with Oscietra caviar; and in the surprising tropical notes of a blue lobster salad with green mango.

Homage to Pierre Soulages.

"Just before the restaurant closed due to the lockdown, we had made bread with vegetable charcoal. I prepared it like a 'croque-monsieur', alternating layers of bread and Comté."

And although less apparent at first glance, his discovery of Japan would play a decisive role in the refinement of his cuisine. In the Land of the Rising Sun, he met extraordinarily rigorous cooks and discovered a new perspective on the use of certain ingredients and the way flavours can be combined.

There, as in Illhaeusern, eras intertwine, and cuisine—like the poetry of haiku—builds bridges between the many emotions that give our human experience its flavour: past sentiments and present desires, the fleeting and the enduring, the boldness of progress and respect for tradition.

His artist's soul can then reconnect with the fragility of the seasons and with the conversations about nature he had as a child with Madame Zimmer, an anthroposophist disciple of Rudolf Steiner with whom he boarded in Ribeauvillé. And with his long wanderings in the forest.

His sensitivity surfaces in dishes such as Vosges ceps cooked with fig leaves, hay-roasted eel, or mackerel with white wine and daikon, where his cuisine takes on a deep, irresistible resonance, attuning itself to the song of the world around him. This sense of time—elusive as a shimmer on the surface of water—is one that Marc Haeberlin nevertheless succeeds in capturing with a painter's delicacy.

The waters of the Ill flowing through his veins then assume another dimension. No longer do they carry heritage and tradition alone; they become whisper and light. They suffuse the walls of the Auberge and transcend the interior design conceived by Patrick Jouin and Sanjit Manku. Encircled by a forest of reeds, three rings of polished stainless steel with a hammered surface allow it to radiate in majesty across the restaurant tables. Filtered through the ethereal draperies, the tireless clarity of this river-time — gliding beneath the broad bay windows — fills the rooms with its serenity.

Meats

Beef Blade in Pinot Noir with Stuffed Marrow Bone

Serves 4

1 piece blade of beef (1 kg)
1 onion
2 carrots
1 garlic clove
1 sprig thyme
1 bay leaf
1 pinch Espelette pepper
1 tbsp tomato purée
1 veal foot
1 bottle Alsace Pinot Noir
2 litres veal stock
3 tbsp olive oil

For the marrow bones
4 marrow bones, cut into 2-cm sections
1 bunch parsley
1 shallot
¼ garlic clove
20 g butter
100 g breadcrumbs
Salt, pepper

Preheat the oven to 200°C (th. 6/7). Peel the onion, carrots, and garlic, and cut them into large pieces.

Heat a cast-iron pot with the olive oil and brown the piece of beef on all sides over high heat. Add the aromatic garnish—onion, carrots, thyme, bay leaf, garlic, Espelette pepper, tomato purée—and the veal foot. Deglaze everything with the Pinot Noir, then add the veal stock and one glass of water. Cover the pot and bake for about 30 minutes. Reduce the oven temperature to 150°C (th. 5) and continue cooking for at least 3 hours.

Meanwhile, prepare the marrow bones: blanch them for 3 to 4 minutes in boiling salted water. Allow to cool slightly. Wash, dry, and chop the parsley. Peel and finely chop the shallot; peel and chop the garlic. Sweat the chopped shallot and garlic in the butter. Empty the marrow bones. In a mixer, blend the breadcrumbs, shallot, garlic, beef marrow, and chopped parsley; season with salt and pepper. Stuff the marrow bones with this mixture.

At the end of the beef's cooking, cook the stuffed marrow bones under the oven grill for 5 to 7 minutes, until nicely browned.

Check the cooking of the veal foot and the beef with the tip of a knife. Remove the bones from the veal foot and cut the meat into cubes. Strain the sauce, add the veal-foot cubes, and adjust the seasoning. Cut the beef into large cubes and coat them with the reduced sauce.

Serve the stuffed marrow bones separately, accompanied by a good mashed potato or fresh pasta.

MEATS 131

Whole Roasted Veal Kidneys in Fat with Madeira Sauce and Timut Pepper

Serves 4

- 4 whole veal kidneys, in fat
- 4 tbsp crushed Timut pepper
- 1 garlic clove
- 30 g butter
- 800 g spinach
- Fleur de sel

For the Madeira sauce

- 1 shallot
- 60 g butter
- 30 g flour
- 100 ml Madeira wine
- 250 ml dark veal stock
- Slightly thickened with roux

Preheat the oven to 230°C (th. 8/9). Using a knife, remove the excess fat around the kidneys, taking care to leave them wrapped in their natural fat. Rub each kidney with crushed Timut pepper and a little fleur de sel.

Place the kidneys in a baking dish and roast for 20 to 25 minutes until nicely coloured. Let them cool, covered with aluminium foil.

Meanwhile, prepare the sauce. Peel and finely chop the shallot. Prepare the roux by cooking 30 g of butter and the flour together in a saucepan. Sweat the chopped shallot in 30 g of butter, then moisten with the Madeira wine and the veal stock. Simmer for 20 minutes.

Peel and chop the garlic. In a pot, melt 30 g of butter, add the garlic and the washed spinach. Cover and cook for about 2 minutes, then drain to remove excess moisture.

Reheat the kidneys in the oven for 5 minutes, then slice them. On each plate, arrange the spinach and place the kidney slices on top.

Serve the sauce on the side, and sprinkle the kidneys with a little fleur de sel if desired. These kidneys are best served with spätzle (recipe on page 137).

MEATS 135

Alsatian Spätzle

Serves 8

500 g flour
4 eggs + 2 yolks
250 ml water
100 g butter
Nutmeg
Salt

Place the flour in a mixing bowl. Add the whole eggs, the yolks, the water, a pinch of salt, and a little freshly grated nutmeg. Work the dough well, incorporating air, until it no longer sticks to the sides of the bowl. The dough should be fairly thick.

Bring a pot of salted water to the boil. Spread a little dough onto a wooden board. Using a damp spatula, cut thin strips of dough and let them fall into the boiling water.

As soon as the spätzle rise to the surface, transfer them to a bowl of cold water. Drain in a colander, then sauté them in butter in a frying pan for a few minutes until lightly browned.

To shape the spätzle, you can also use a colander and a scraper.

Left : Yannis Huet.
Above, from left to right: Floriane Schuller, Anne-Catherine Delorme, Danielle Baumann (Marc's sister), and Patrick Zuccolin (head maître d'hôtel).

Veal Sweetbreads

Recipe created in 1967 on the occasion of the twinning of Illhaeusern with Collonges-au-Mont-d'Or, where Paul Bocuse's restaurant is located

Serves 4

- 2 veal sweetbreads (400 g each)
- 1 onion
- 1 garlic clove
- 2 carrots
- ¼ celeriac
- 1 handful parsley stems
- 1 sprig thyme
- ½ bay leaf
- 250 ml Riesling
- 40 ml Noilly Prat
- 250 ml light veal stock
- 60 g butter
- Salt, pepper

For the sauce

- 300 g julienned vegetables (carrot, leek whites, a little celery)
- 1 truffle (50 g)
- 250 ml double cream
- 1 tbsp roux (see page 179)
- Juice of ½ lemon
- Salt, pepper

Soak the veal sweetbreads in cold water overnight. Then blanch them for 3 to 4 minutes in boiling salted water. Cool them and remove the cartilage.

Peel and slice the onion; peel and roughly cut the carrots and the celery.

Generously butter a casserole and add the sliced onion, the vegetables, the parsley stems, the unpeeled garlic clove, the thyme, and the bay leaf. Place the sweetbreads on top of the vegetables. Moisten with the Riesling, the Noilly Prat, and the light veal stock. Simmer covered for 20 minutes, ensuring that the vegetables do not brown.

For the sauce, sweat in butter the julienned carrot, leek whites, a little celery, and the truffle slices. Keep warm after cooking.

Remove the sweetbreads to a serving dish and strain the cooking liquid through a chinois, pressing well. Pour the liquid into a sauté pan, add the double cream, and reduce over medium heat for about 5 minutes. Thicken with the roux. Adjust the seasoning, add the lemon juice, and the julienned vegetables and truffle.

Coat the sweetbreads with this sauce and serve with noodles.

Pig's Trotter Stuffed with Truffle

Serves 4

2 pig's trotters
200 g cooked Tarbais beans
(soaked 10 hours the day before)
2 onions
2 carrots
1 piece celeriac, 70 g + 10 g
1 leek + 1 leek white
1 bouquet garni
150 ml white wine
1 truffle (40 g)
2 tbsp chopped flat-leaf parsley
400 g pork caul fat
100 g flour
2 eggs
100 g breadcrumbs
50 g butter
2 tbsp sunflower oil
300 ml Périgueux sauce
Sherry vinegar
Salt, pepper

For the stuffing

100 g poultry meat
50 g boneless pork shoulder
100 g pork back fat
20 g chicken liver
1 egg
1 tbsp cognac
1 tbsp port
1 tbsp truffle juice
Salt, pepper

Peel one onion, one carrot, and half of the celeriac. Clean the whole leek. Place the pig's trotters in a cast-iron pot with these vegetables and the bouquet garni. Cover with water, add the white wine, and lightly salt. Bring to the boil, cover, and cook for 2 to 2½ hours. Let the trotters cool in their cooking liquid.

Remove the trotters from the broth and debone them carefully, removing all the small cartilages. Place the meat in a bowl and season with pepper. Chop the truffle and add it along with the parsley. Mix and press everything firmly into a rectangular terrine. Refrigerate overnight.

The next day, soak the caul fat in cold water. Remove the preparation from the terrine and cut it into large blocks, about 4 cm × 8 cm.

Prepare the stuffing: pass all the meats through a meat grinder fitted with the medium plate. Incorporate the egg, cognac, port, and truffle juice. Mix with a spatula. Season with salt and pepper.

Preheat the oven to 200°C (th. 6/7). Drain the caul fat and unfold it carefully. Cut into squares of about 15 cm.

Spread a thin layer of stuffing over one square, place a cold trotter block in the centre, and roll the caul fat to form a cylinder.

Beat the egg with a fork. Dip the cylinders successively in flour, egg, and breadcrumbs. Heat the oil and butter in a pan and brown the breaded cylinders on all sides for 5 minutes. Transfer to the oven for 15 minutes, then leave them in the warm oven for 10 minutes so they become very crisp.

Peel the remaining onion and vegetables. Finely chop the onion; cut the carrot, celeriac, and the white of the leek into brunoise. Sweat them in a sauté pan with a knob of butter. Reheat this ragout. Add a dash of sherry vinegar and adjust seasoning.

Reheat the Périgueux sauce. Serve the pig's trotters piping hot with the Périgueux sauce and Tarbais beans.

Pigeon Tournedos with Cabbage and Truffle

Serves 4

4 pigeon supremes, boned
4 slices raw foie gras (30 g each)
1 tbsp cognac
2 tbsp port
2 large Savoy cabbage leaves
400 g pork caul fat
4 slices truffle
1 tbsp peanut oil
Salt, pepper

For the stuffing
50 g boneless pork shoulder
100 g pork back fat
20 g raw goose foie gras
50 g poultry livers
1 shallot
1 tbsp cognac
1 tbsp port
1 tbsp truffle juice
1 egg
10 g butter
Salt, pepper

Place the pigeon supremes and the foie gras slices on a plate, add the cognac and port. Season with salt and pepper and let marinate for 20 minutes at room temperature.

Prepare the stuffing: peel and chop the shallot, then sweat it in the butter for 3 minutes. Clean the poultry livers. Pass through a meat grinder fitted with the medium plate the pork shoulder, pork fat, foie gras, poultry livers, and the shallot. Add the spirits, truffle juice, egg, salt, and pepper. Mix thoroughly.

Cut the cabbage leaves in half, removing the central rib. Blanch them for 2 minutes in boiling salted water, then cool under cold water and pat dry.

Drain the caul fat, unfold it carefully, and spread it on the work surface. Cut 4 squares of about 20 cm. Spread each square with a thin layer of stuffing using a stainless-steel spatula, leaving a bit of caul fat overhanging. Place on top ½ cabbage leaf, 1 slice of foie gras, 1 slice of truffle, and 1 pigeon supreme. Wrap with the cabbage leaf, then roll in the caul fat. The stuffing should cover everything. Tighten the caul fat well to form a compact ball. Prepare 4 elongated balls this way.

Preheat the oven to 210°C (th. 7). Place the balls in an oiled baking dish. Slide the dish into the oven and cook for 5 minutes. At the end of the cooking time, switch off the oven and let the tournedos rest inside for 10 minutes, door slightly open, after which cut each ball in half.

Serve the pigeon tournedos hot, reheated with a little melted butter, surrounded with Périgueux sauce and, if desired, some shredded green cabbage.

MEATS

Miéral Bresse Chicken, Poached Demi-Deuil

Serves 4

1 fine Miéral Bresse chicken (2 kg), not cleaned
1 truffle (50 g)
5 litres white poultry stock
1 onion
4 large new carrots with tops
4 leeks
1 celeriac
4 large potatoes
Salt, pepper

For the vinaigrette
1 tsp mustard
100 ml extra-virgin olive oil
3 tbsp balsamic vinegar

Clean the chicken, then contise it: slip one slice of truffle under the skin of each thigh and each breast without tearing the skin.

Heat the white poultry stock in a large pot. Immerse the truffled, trussed chicken. Season with salt and pepper and add the peeled onion. Cook for 1 hour at a gentle simmer.

Meanwhile, peel the carrots, leaving 1–2 cm of the tops attached. Clean the leeks and tie them into bundles with kitchen string. Peel and cut the celeriac into eight pieces. Peel the potatoes. Cook all the vegetables separately in the stock, checking their doneness carefully with the tip of a knife.

In a blender, place the mustard, olive oil, balsamic vinegar, and 2 ladlefuls of hot chicken stock. Blend everything together and serve the warm vinaigrette in a sauceboat.

Arrange the vegetables on a serving platter with the chicken in the centre. Carve the bird in front of the guests.

Viennese Escalope as My Grandmother Used to Make It

This dish is, for me, a Proust madeleine. It was my grandmother, Marie Ittel, who gave me my first education in taste through these cutlets

Serves 4

- 4 large veal cutlets (200 g each)
- 1 egg
- 1 pinch Espelette pepper
- 4 tbsp flour
- 400 g fine breadcrumbs made from dried white bread without the crust
- 100 ml peanut oil
- 1 tbsp goose fat or butter
- 2 lemons
- Salt, pepper

Pound the cutlets thoroughly using a rolling pin. Beat the egg with a fork in a deep plate and season with salt and Espelette pepper.

Dredge the cutlets in flour, tapping off any excess. Dip them into the beaten egg, then coat them in the breadcrumbs. Press the breadcrumbs on well with your hand, then score a light crosshatch pattern on both sides using the back of a large knife.

Heat the oil and goose fat or butter in a frying pan. Brown the breaded cutlets for about 4 minutes on each side until they develop a beautiful golden colour.

Remove and drain on paper towels. Salt very lightly.

Prepare the historiated lemons, meaning cut them in half in a zigzag pattern.

Serve with the zigzag-cut lemon halves, along with a good green salad and sautéed potatoes.

Traditional Stuffed Duckling

Serves 4

1 Challans duckling (1 kg), cleaned
1 large carrot
2 courgettes
12 pearl onions
12 Ratte potatoes
40 ml dry white wine
½ litre chicken stock
1 garlic clove
1 sprig thyme
Salt, pepper

For the stuffing

1 small bread roll
1 bunch basil
1 shallot
2 pale poultry livers
100 g pork back fat
1 chicken breast
1 egg
Milk
Salt, pepper

Soak the small bread roll in a little milk. Wash, dry, and remove the basil leaves; set a few aside for serving. Peel the shallot.

In a bowl, pass through a meat grinder fitted with the fine plate the soaked bread, the bunch of basil, the shallot, the poultry livers, the pork back fat, and the chicken breast. Season and add the egg. Mix thoroughly.

Season the inside of the duckling with salt and pepper. Stuff it with the filling and truss it with a needle.

Peel the carrot and the courgettes, then cut them into oblique slices. Peel the onions. Blanch the Ratte potatoes for 15 minutes in salted water, then peel them as soon as they are cool enough to handle.

Preheat the oven to 200°C (th. 6/7). Season the duckling and place it in a cast-iron cocotte. Roast uncovered for 15 minutes, then cover and cook for 1 hour 25 minutes, lowering the oven temperature to 160°C (th. 5/6) after 1 hour of cooking.

When this cooking time is over, remove the rendered fat from the cocotte, then add the white wine, chicken stock, all the vegetables, the unpeeled garlic clove, and the thyme. Cook everything for an additional 20 minutes. Adjust the seasoning of the jus if necessary.

Serve everything directly in the cast-iron cocotte. Garnish with a few basil leaves.

Photo of the recipe on the next page

Veal Shank Marrakech-Inspired

Serves 4

1 veal shank (front)
1 tbsp Espelette pepper
1 tbsp ras el hanout
2 large carrots
2 courgettes
1 aubergine
500 g Ratte potatoes
1 litre veal stock
1 head garlic
1 sprig thyme
1 bay leaf
1 pinch saffron threads
Peel of 1 salt-preserved lemon
40 ml extra-virgin olive oil
80 g butter
Salt, pepper

Salt the veal shank and rub it with Espelette pepper and ras el hanout. Heat a casserole with a drizzle of olive oil and brown the shank over high heat on all sides.

Meanwhile, peel the carrots; leave the skin on the courgettes and the aubergine; cut the vegetables into 2 or 3 equal-sized pieces. Brown the Ratte potatoes in a pan with a little butter.

Preheat the oven to 180°C (th. 6). Place the shank in the casserole, cover, and bake with the veal stock, a glass of water, the halved head of garlic, thyme, bay leaf, and a pinch of saffron for 1 hour and 15 minutes.

At the end of this cooking time, add all the vegetables and potatoes to the casserole and continue cooking for 30 to 35 minutes. Then add the preserved lemon peel cut into wedges. Adjust seasoning at the end of cooking.

Serve directly in the casserole or arrange everything in a tagine dish.

MEATS 157

Above: Guillaume Schuller, kitchen sous-chef, at the pass

Brasserie des Haras Choucroute Garnie

Recipe by François Baur, head chef of the brasserie

Serves 6 to 8

2 kg sauerkraut
2 salted pork knuckles
1 smoked schiffala (pork shoulder)
500 g smoked bacon
250 g salted bacon
6 Knack sausages
6 smoked Montbéliard sausages
6 small boudin noir
2 onions
1 garlic clove
100 g goose fat
20 juniper berries
500 ml white wine
Salt

For the spice bag
(1 small linen bag)
1 sprig thyme
1 bay leaf
1 clove
A few crushed coriander seeds
A few crushed black peppercorns
1 tbsp black caraway seeds

Soak the schiffala and the salted bacon in cold water overnight to remove excess salt.

Rinse the sauerkraut in warm water and drain it in a colander. Squeeze it well with your hands (if it is not new-season sauerkraut).

Cook the meats and the bacon in a saucepan of boiling water for about 30 minutes.

Preheat the oven to 180°C (th. 6). Peel and slice the onions; peel the garlic clove.

In a large casserole dish, heat the goose fat and sweat the sliced onions. Add the sauerkraut, the juniper berries, the crushed garlic clove and the small linen bag containing the spices.

Moisten with the white wine and some of the meat cooking liquid, adding salt only if necessary. Cover and allow to simmer in the oven for 1 hour and 30 minutes. Halfway through cooking, add the meats and the bacon. The sauerkraut should remain slightly firm to the bite.

In the meat cooking water, poach the sausages. Briefly fry the small boudin noir in a frying pan.

When cooked, remove the meats and bacon. Adjust the seasoning of the sauerkraut and arrange it in an earthenware dish, placing the meat, bacon, sausages and fried boudin noir around it.

Serve with potatoes cooked in their skins or Ratte potatoes.

Herb-Roasted Rack of Lamb

Serves 4

2 racks of lamb, trimmed and frenched
200 ml lamb jus (recipe below)
2 garlic cloves
1 sprig rosemary
40 ml olive oil
Salt, pepper

For 500 ml lamb jus

1 kg lamb trimmings, bones or neck
1 onion
2 shallots
1 head garlic
20 ml olive oil
1 tbsp tomato purée
100 ml white wine
1 litre white poultry stock
1 sprig thyme
1 small bay leaf
1 tomato

Preheat the oven to 220°C (th. 7/8). Brown the racks of lamb in a frying pan with the olive oil, then roast them in the oven for 12 minutes with the unpeeled garlic cloves and the rosemary.

Cover the racks with aluminium foil and leave the meat to rest at room temperature for 10 minutes.

Reheat the lamb jus and adjust the seasoning.

For the lamb jus

Peel the onion and the shallots and cut them into large pieces. Separate the garlic cloves without peeling them.

In a cast-iron casserole, brown the lamb trimmings with the onion and the shallots over a medium heat in a little oil. When they reach a regular blond colour, add the unpeeled garlic cloves and allow to brown for a further 15 minutes.

Transfer everything to a colander to drain and remove the fat from the casserole. Place the spoonful of tomato purée into the casserole, return the lamb trimmings, and deglaze over a high heat with the wine. Reduce until dry.

Add 500 ml water and scrape up all the caramelised juices from the bottom of the casserole with a spatula, then reduce by three-quarters over a low heat, coating the lamb well, for about 20 minutes.

Add the white stock, thyme, bay leaf and chopped tomato, and simmer for about 1 hour and 30 minutes until the jus becomes syrupy. Strain through a fine chinois.

Serve the rack of lamb and its sauce with potatoes cooked Munster-valley style with black olives and thyme (recipe on the next page).

Potatoes Cooked Munster-Valley Style with Black Olives and Thyme

Serves 4 to 6

500 g floury potatoes
50 g pitted black olives in oil
1 onion
1 garlic clove
150 ml dry white wine
500 ml white poultry stock
1 large sprig fresh thyme
1 tbsp thick cream
5 tbsp olive oil
50 g butter
Salt, pepper

Preheat the oven to 180°C (th. 6). Peel the potatoes, wash them, and cut them into pieces. Halve the olives. Peel the onion and the garlic and slice them.

Heat the olive oil in a cast-iron casserole and gently soften the onion and garlic over a low heat for 2 minutes.

Add the potatoes, season with salt and pepper, and mix well. Pour in the white wine and scrape the bottom of the casserole with a spatula to loosen the cooking juices.

Allow to reduce for a few minutes, then add the poultry stock. Add the thyme. Cover the casserole, place it in the oven, and cook for 1 hour.

Remove the casserole from the oven and take out the thyme. Mash the potatoes using a wooden spatula. Add the olives, the cream, the remaining oil, and the butter cut into pieces. Serve immediately.

This is a perfect accompaniment for lamb

WATER MOVEMENT

The Ill of The Family

Heir to four generations of cooks, a chef of masterful talent recognised and celebrated by his peers, Marc Haeberlin nevertheless measures his deepest sense of accomplishment by another standard: the fulfilment of all those who contribute each day to enhance the aura of the Auberge de l'Ill. Listening with sincerity, caring for everyone's aspirations, training, instilling confidence, setting aside preconceptions, developing new talents and new specialities – these are daily actions that reinforce and broaden the family spirit of the Auberge and prepare it to face the challenges of its future.

Within this constellation of talents and personalities, there is Laetitia, Marc's eldest daughter, discreet and efficient, who oversees the reception of guests. There is Danielle, Marc's sister, her husband Marco Baumann, and their two children, Salomé and Édouard, who are responsible for the hospitality of the restaurant and the adjoining Hôtel des Berges. A five-star haven with eighteen rooms and an 800-square-metre spa, it gently extends the gastronomic experience.

An experience that would doubtless not be so singular without the dedication of these teams, who infuse the warm atmosphere of the Auberge with their expertise and good humour. In the dining room, alongside Stéphane Laruelle, Laurent Schneider and Patrick Zuccolin, the maîtres d'hôtel, and the sommeliers Hervé Fleuriel, Frédéric Schaetzel and Serge Dubs (World's Best Sommelier in 1989), nearly twenty people work together to ensure the seamless choreography of each service.

Opposite: Jean-Paul Bostoen (Meilleur Ouvrier de France 2011), Marc Haeberlin's head chef.

In the kitchen, Marc Haeberlin's right-hand man is Jean-Paul Bostoen. Having joined the Auberge in 2002, this Meilleur Ouvrier de France coordinates, together with his sous-chef Guillaume Schuller, the work of a brigade of around twenty cooks. In the pastry section, it is chef Pascal Hainigue—who returned to Alsace in 2023 after several successful Parisian experiences at the George V, the Bristol and the Burgundy—who leads his team, supported by Francis Bellicam and Hugo Loisel.

Under their guidance, the pastry creations have also evolved in line with contemporary tastes: less sugar, more fruity or chocolate-driven sensations (rhubarb meringue tart, rhubarb baba with gin and verbena, etc.), while preserving cornerstone indulgences such as the celebrated Haeberlin peach or the vanilla–raspberry iced vacherin prepared just as grandmother Marthe used to make it.

Guided by Marc Haeberlin's humanist values and strong sense of collective endeavour, these teams form a passionate and supportive environment in which the next generation of great French and international establishments is trained—whether heirs to a tradition or unexpected new talents.

This is the case of Thierno Ousmane Bah, a young man from Guinea-Conakry, who arrived through the association Épices founded by Isabelle Haeberlin, Marc's wife. Based in Mulhouse, the association works to support the social and professional integration of young and older people alike through employment in the kitchen.

For—perhaps most importantly—the living spirit of the Auberge continues to spread irresistibly and to branch out. In Nagoya, Tokyo and Sapporo since 2007, in collaboration with chef Taichi Nakahiro, but also since 2013 in Strasbourg at the Brasserie des Haras, opened under the initiative of Professor Jacques Marescaux and run by Maxime, one of Marc and Isabelle Haeberlin's sons. In this major institution, chef François Baur, trained at the Auberge de l'Ill, offers a variety of brasserie dishes, including certain regional treasures such as the unmissable choucroute.

A story that continues to be written and will soon extend to the slopes of the Ribeauvillé vineyard with the 2027 opening of the Clos Saint-Vincent, a hotel (33 rooms) and restaurant project led by the couple's three children—Laetitia, Xavier and Maxime—and whose interior design has been entrusted to Patrick Jouin and Sanjit Manku.

The next step in a family adventure that continues to unfold with the flow of the water, linking the islands one by one into a constellation of stars.

Game

Spice-Lacquered Mallard

Serves 4

2 mallards, plucked, gutted and trussed
2 garlic cloves
3 cm fresh ginger root
4 green cardamom pods
30 g Sichuan pepper
30 g coriander seeds
30 g cumin seeds
150 g acacia honey
1 tbsp soy sauce
1 tbsp dry sherry
Salt, pepper

For the duck jus
6 duck wings
2 shallots
100 ml port
500 ml white stock
10 g butter
10 g flour
Salt, pepper

Peel the garlic cloves. Peel the ginger and cut it in half.

Remove the cardamom seeds from their pods. Using a grinder, reduce the cardamom, Sichuan pepper, coriander and cumin to a powder. Mix this powder with the honey, soy sauce and sherry. Add the whole garlic cloves and the ginger. Keep this mixture at room temperature for 1 week to allow all the aromas to infuse properly.

Preheat the oven to 210°C (th. 7). Crush the duck wings reserved for the jus and place them in a roasting tin. Season the ducks inside and out. Using a brush, coat the ducks with the spiced honey, reserving about 2 tablespoons of the mixture. Place the ducks on top of the wings. Roast for 20 minutes, until they are nicely golden.

Remove the tin from the oven, take out the ducks, and leave them to rest for 15 minutes.

Meanwhile, prepare the duck jus: peel the shallots and cut them into eight. Place them in a saucepan or sauté pan and roast over a medium heat for 5 minutes. Add the port, reduce to a syrup, then scrape the bottom of the tin with a spatula. To dissolve the cooking juices, pour in the white stock. Reduce by half for 10 minutes.

Make a roux: melt the butter in a small saucepan, add the flour, and stir for 1 minute. Strain the contents of the roasting tin through a fine sieve, return the jus to the heat, add the roux, mix well, and simmer gently for a further 10 minutes. Adjust the seasoning.

After the 15-minute resting time, brush the ducks again with the reserved honey. Return them to the oven and reheat for 6 minutes.

To serve, remove the breasts from the ducks and slice them into strips. Serve piping hot with red cabbage, maize galettes, and the duck jus in a sauceboat.

To accompany this dish, see the recipe for red cabbage confit with figs (page 91).

Photo of the recipe on the next page

Roast Pheasant on Sauerkraut

Serves 4

1 pheasant, gutted and trussed
2 shallots
2 onions
250 ml dry white wine
250 ml dark stock thickened with roux
80 g goose or duck fat
200 g smoked bacon
500 g sauerkraut
1 pinch black caraway
6 juniper berries
1 bay leaf
120 g butter
20 ml olive oil
Salt, pepper

For the roux
30 g butter
30 g flour

Preheat the oven to 220°C (th. 7/8). Season the pheasant with salt and pepper, place it in a casserole, brush it with olive oil, add 50 g butter and brown it on all sides. Then roast for about 35 minutes. After cooking, remove it and leave it to rest wrapped in aluminium foil.

Meanwhile, peel and finely chop the shallots and onions.

Prepare the roux by browning the butter and flour together in a saucepan.

In the casserole, sweat the shallots in butter, pour in a quarter of the white wine, reduce, add the dark stock, and simmer for 20 minutes, then whisk in 50 g cold butter. Keep this sauce warm.

In another casserole, sweat the sliced onions in the goose fat. Add the smoked bacon, the washed and drained sauerkraut (unless it is new-season), the spices and aromatics, the remaining white wine, and 1-2 glasses of water. Season with salt and pepper, cover, and cook in the oven for 50 minutes to 1 hour.

Reheat the pheasant in the oven to make it crisp, carve it, and arrange it over the hot sauerkraut.

Serve the sauce separately in a sauceboat.

Venison Medallions with Chartreuse Sauce

Serves 4

½ saddle of venison, 1 kg
150 g butter
2 tbsp tomato purée
1 bouquet garni
2 tbsp Chartreuse
50 ml cognac
1 tbsp redcurrant jelly
Salt, pepper

For the marinade
750 ml red wine
1 onion
1 small carrot
1 sprig parsley
1 small sprig thyme
½ bay leaf
1 clove
1 sprig rosemary
6 juniper berries

For the garnish
2 reinette apples
500 ml white wine
250 g wild mushrooms
20 g butter
100 g lingonberry or blueberry jam
Salt, pepper

Skin and bone the saddle of venison. Peel the onion and carrot and cut them into a mirepoix. Marinate the venison fillets in a good red-wine marinade with the onion and carrot mirepoix, the parsley, thyme, bay leaf, clove, rosemary and juniper berries. Leave in the marinade for 1 hour.

Prepare a game stock: sauté the chopped carcass and trimmings of the saddle in 20 g butter, then add the drained mirepoix from the marinade. Allow everything to brown well, then moisten with the marinade, add the tomato purée and the bouquet garni. Simmer uncovered for 1 hour and 30 minutes, skimming regularly. Strain the stock through a fine sieve.

Cut the fillets into 8 medallions (pieces 2–3 cm thick), season with salt and pepper. Sauté them in 20 g butter, keeping them slightly pink. Deglaze the sauté pan with the cognac and add the game stock. Whisk in 110 g butter. Add the redcurrant jelly, then the Chartreuse. Mix and adjust the seasoning.

For the garnish, halve and core the apples. Poach the half-apples in white wine for 10 minutes in a saucepan. In a frying pan, sauté the mushrooms in butter for a few minutes over a high heat.

Arrange the venison medallions on a hot dish and coat them with the sauce. Place on one side the apples filled with lingonberry or blueberry jam, and on the other side the sautéed mushrooms.

Serve with knepfle (Alsatian pasta) with fromage blanc.

Photo of the recipe overleaf

Partridge Romanov

Serves 4

4 young partridges
4 tbsp port
1 tbsp cognac
100 g caul fat
4 slices goose liver
4 slices truffle
Butter for the dish
Salt, pepper

For the sauce
1 onion
1 carrot
250 ml white wine
125 ml veal stock
1 tomato
1 sprig thyme
6 juniper berries
100 ml thick cream
50 g butter
Salt, pepper

For the stuffing
100 g pork
100 g back fat
50 g poultry livers
2 shallots
25 g butter
1 egg yolk
1 pinch spiced salt
1 tbsp truffle juice

Prepare the partridges by removing the innards. Set aside the livers and hearts. Bone the breasts, remove the skin, and keep the legs whole with the thighs, trimming off the claws. Marinate the suprêmes with the port and the cognac. Season with salt and pepper.

For the sauce: peel the onion and carrot, then cut them into a mirepoix.

In a saucepan, brown the partridge bones with the onion and carrot. Deglaze with the white wine, the veal stock and the marinade from the suprêmes. Add the tomato cut into four pieces, the thyme and the juniper berries. Simmer gently for 1 hour until the stock becomes syrupy.

Prepare the stuffing: peel and finely chop the shallots, then sweat them in butter.

Pass the pork, the back fat, the poultry livers and the partridge livers and hearts through a meat grinder fitted with the fine plate. Mix well in a bowl with the shallots, the egg yolk, the spiced salt and the truffle juice.

Preheat the oven to 200°C (th. 6/7).

Prepare the cutlets: spread the caul fat on a board. Cut it into 4 rectangles of 15–20 cm.

Spread a thin layer of stuffing on each rectangle. Place the partridge leg at one end, followed by the partridge suprême, a slice of truffle and a piece of raw goose liver. Cover with another thin layer of stuffing. Shape each into a cutlet, using the partridge leg as the "bone".

Place the cutlets in a buttered dish and roast for 14 minutes. The breasts should remain slightly pink. Let them rest for 5 minutes after coming out of the oven.

Finish the sauce: while the cutlets are roasting, strain the stock through a fine sieve, then add the thick cream and the butter in small pieces. Arrange the cutlets on a serving dish. Adjust the seasoning of the sauce and pour it over the cutlets.

Serve with stuffed cabbage and Maxim potatoes.

Lièvre à la Royale

Serves 8 to 10

1 hare, 3 kg
1 goose liver, 400 g
60 ml cognac
Salt, pepper

For the marinade

3 onions
4 garlic cloves
2 carrots
1 bottle red wine
1 sprig thyme
1 bay leaf
2 cloves
1 handful parsley stalks

For the stuffing

2 small bread rolls
250 ml milk
100 g pork back fat
200 g pork meat
200 g hare meat (not marinated)
2 shallots
1–2 garlic cloves
1 egg
A dash of cognac
Spiced salt

For the sauce

80 g butter
2 tbsp flour
1 bottle red wine
500 ml beef or veal stock
2 tbsp tomato purée
1 bouquet garni
Salt, pepper

Skin the hare, or have your game dealer do it for you.

Reserve the liver, the heart and the blood. Place the blood in a bowl and completely bone the hare. Peel the onions, garlic and carrots and cut them roughly. Mix all the marinade ingredients and marinate the hare and its bones for 12 hours in the refrigerator.

Season the goose liver with salt and pepper and marinate it with the cognac.

Soak the bread rolls in a little milk. Peel, finely chop and sweat the shallots in butter. Peel and chop the garlic. Prepare the stuffing by passing all the meats and the soaked bread through a meat grinder fitted with the fine plate. Place in a bowl. Add the egg, the shallots, the garlic, the spiced salt and the cognac. Mix the stuffing thoroughly.

Lay the hare flat on its back on a large tea towel; season with salt and pepper. Spread a layer of stuffing inside and place the goose liver, cut lengthways into four, in the centre. Cover with more stuffing. Fold the hare's meat over the stuffing. Wrap it in the tea towel and roll it into a large cylinder. Tie it tightly.

In a large casserole, brown the hare bones and the vegetables from the marinade in butter. Sprinkle with flour and moisten with the marinade, the bottle of red wine and the stock. Add the tomato purée and the bouquet garni.

Preheat the oven to 200°C (th. 6/7). Place the hare, wrapped in the cloth, into the casserole. It must be completely covered with the cooking liquid. Cook in the oven for 2 hours and 30 minutes.

Remove the casserole, take off the cloth, and keep the hare warm.

At the last moment, thicken the sauce with the blood. Bring it to a bare simmer and stop as soon as the first bubble appears. Pass everything through a fine sieve. Adjust the seasoning.

Cut the stuffed hare into thick slices. Arrange on a serving dish and coat with the sauce. Serve with homemade noodles or spätzle.

Photo of the recipe overleaf

GAME 191

Right: Thierno Ousmane Bah.

Woodcock Pie (Club des 100)

Serves 8 to 10

**Woodcock may not be sold.
This dish can only be prepared if a hunter gives you a woodcock.**

2 plucked woodcocks with heads
120 g raw foie gras (duck or goose)
1 fresh truffle
100 ml port
100 ml cognac
1 shallot
1 litre red wine
1 garlic clove
1 litre game stock
500 g all-butter puff pastry
1 egg for glazing
100 g butter
30 ml olive oil
Salt, pepper

For the stuffing
50 g sliced white bread
250 ml milk
500 g pork shoulder
50 g poultry meat
1 egg
4 poultry livers
Salt, pepper

Cut up the woodcocks, removing the meat from the breasts and thighs, then cut the meat, the raw foie gras and the truffle into large cubes. Season with salt, pepper, a little port and cognac. Leave to marinate in the refrigerator for 1 to 2 hours.

Collect all the entrails of the woodcocks, including the intestines and gizzards, and chop everything very finely with a knife. Peel and finely chop the shallot. Sweat it in a little butter, add the chopped entrails, season with salt and pepper, then deglaze with port, cognac and a little red wine. Add the peeled garlic clove, reduce and cook for 15 minutes. Set aside and chill.

Soak the sliced white bread in a little milk.

Pass all the ingredients for the stuffing through a meat grinder fitted with the fine plate. Mix in half of the chilled entrail mixture and the marinated meats. Chill for at least 1 hour.

Crush the woodcock bones, brown them in olive oil in a saucepan, then moisten with red wine, the remaining cognac and port, and the game stock. Simmer for at least 1 hour, then strain the stock, add the remaining entrail mixture and whisk in the remaining butter.

Roll out a sheet of puff pastry, not too thin, and place it in a high-sided, non-stick or buttered tart tin. Place the woodcock stuffing in the centre. Brush the edges with beaten egg. Roll out a second disc of puff pastry, cover the pie as for a classic pie, seal the edges, trim away the excess pastry, decorate the top with the tip of a knife, and make a chimney in the centre. Chill for at least 2 hours.

Preheat the oven to 200°C (th. 6/7), then bake the pie for 35 minutes. After baking, place the roasted woodcock head in the chimney at the centre of the pie.

Cut into equal portions. Spoon a little sauce into each plate, then add a slice of the pie. This dish may be served with a green salad.

Carving the woodcock pie

Desserts

Roasted Figs with Fig-Leaf Ice Cream

Serves 4

For the roasted figs
8 fine figs
8 fig leaves
100 g acacia honey
3 cinnamon sticks

For the fig-leaf ice cream
500 ml milk
150 ml whipping cream
25 g milk powder
40 g trimoline
2 g ice-cream stabiliser
120 g caster sugar
65 g egg yolks
10 g fig leaves

For the seed crisp
3 sheets brick pastry
50 g icing sugar
50 g five-seed mix
Butter
Isigny thick cream, to serve

Preheat the oven to 180°C (th. 6). In a dish, lay out 4 fig leaves, place the peeled figs on top, drizzle with the honey, add the cinnamon sticks and the fig peelings, then cover with the remaining 4 fig leaves. Cover with aluminium foil and bake for about 15 minutes.

Finely chop 4 of the figs to make a compôte, then use this compôte to fill the baked figs from the base using a piping bag. Reserve the cooking juices and reduce them until syrupy for glazing the figs.

In a saucepan, heat the milk, cream, milk powder and trimoline with one third of the sugar. At 40°C, add the stabiliser mixed with another third of the sugar, then bring to the boil. Pour the hot mixture over the egg yolks, previously blanched with the remaining third of the sugar, and cook as a custard (à l'anglaise) at 85°C for about 10 minutes, stirring constantly with a wooden spoon. Add the finely sliced fig leaves. Leave the ice-cream base to mature overnight, then strain, blend and churn in an ice-cream machine.

Preheat the oven again to 180°C (th. 6). Brush the brick pastry sheets with butter, dust with icing sugar and roll them up. Slice finely to obtain thin strands, place them at the bottom of four tart rings of about 6 cm in diameter, sprinkle with the seed mixture, and bake for about 10 minutes.

Arrange the warm figs on plates and glaze with the reduced cooking juice. Add a quenelle of fig-leaf ice cream and place a seed crisp on top of the quenelle. Serve with a little Isigny thick cream.

Vanilla and Raspberry Iced Vacherin, as My Grandmother Marthe Made It

Serves 8

For the French meringue
200 g egg whites
200 g caster sugar
200 g icing sugar

For the raspberry sorbet
500 g raspberry pulp
100 g caster sugar
5 g stabiliser

For the vanilla ice cream
350 ml milk
150 ml whipping cream
4 Tahitian vanilla pods
85 g caster sugar
120 g egg yolks

For assembly
½ litre whipped cream

Preheat the oven to 130°C (th. 4/5). Using a mixer, whisk the egg whites while gradually adding the caster sugar, then fold in the sifted icing sugar with a spatula.

On a baking tray, pipe two discs 25 cm in diameter using a piping bag fitted with a plain nozzle. Bake for 1 hour.

Prepare the sorbet. In a saucepan, bring the sugar, the stabiliser and 200 ml water to the boil. Cool the syrup, then mix it with the raspberry pulp and churn in the ice-cream maker.

For the vanilla ice cream, bring the milk, cream and the split, scraped vanilla pods to the boil in a saucepan.

In a mixing bowl, beat the egg yolks with the sugar and pour the boiling liquid over them while whisking. Return the mixture to a low heat (or a bain-marie) and cook like a custard at 85°C, for about 10 minutes, stirring constantly with a wooden spoon. Remove from the heat, strain through a fine sieve and churn in the ice-cream maker.

Place the first meringue disc on a serving platter, spread with the vanilla ice cream, then the raspberry sorbet, then top with the second disc and cover the whole vacherin with whipped cream. Freeze for 2 hours.

Remove from the freezer a few minutes before serving and cut the vacherin using a knife dipped in very hot water. It may be served with a raspberry coulis.

You may also prepare individual vacherins, as shown in the photograph.

Cherry Crêpes

Serves 4

1 jar of pitted Griottines in alcohol

For the crêpe batter
400 ml milk
4 eggs
150 g flour
40 g caster sugar
4 g salt
150 g beurre noisette (butter melted and cooked until golden brown)
25 g butter for cooking

For the pastry cream
500 ml milk
15 g butter
1 vanilla pod
40 g egg yolks
100 g caster sugar
40 g crème powder
10 g flour

For the light cream
250 g pastry cream
300 ml very cold whipping cream
20 ml kirsch

Prepare the crêpes. Heat half of the milk. In a mixing bowl, combine the eggs, flour, sugar, salt and the warm milk. Mix well, then add the cold milk, followed by the beurre noisette. Leave the batter to rest in the refrigerator for a few hours before cooking the crêpes in a frying pan with a little butter.

In a saucepan, bring the milk, butter and the split, scraped vanilla pod to the boil. Whisk the egg yolks with the sugar, crème powder and flour. Pour the hot milk over this mixture while whisking, return everything to the saucepan and bring to the boil for 1 minute. Remove from the heat and allow to cool.

Whisk the very cold whipping cream until stiff. Smooth the pastry cream with a whisk, add the kirsch, then gently fold in the whipped cream using a spatula.

On each crêpe, pipe about 50 g of light cream, place 6 Griottines in alcohol on top, and fold the crêpe to form a cushion.

In a saucepan, place 2 filled crêpes per person, add 10 Griottines and some of their alcoholic syrup, then a little kirsch, and finally flambé.

Linzer Tart

Serves 6 to 8

For the Linzer pastry
280 g softened butter
50 g icing sugar
50 g ground almonds
60 g egg yolks
300 g flour
2 g baking powder
12 g ground cinnamon
1 tablespoon dark rum
1 pinch of salt

For the raspberry seed jam
200 g raspberries
200 g caster sugar
200 g unsweetened apple compôte

Prepare the pastry. Mix the softened butter with the icing sugar and the ground almonds. Add the egg yolks along with the remaining ingredients. Gently combine everything until you obtain a smooth, homogeneous dough. Shape into a ball, wrap in cling film and leave to rest overnight in the refrigerator.

In a saucepan, cook the sugar and raspberries until boiling, then add the apple compôte and allow to boil for about 10 minutes. Transfer to a bowl and leave to cool.

Preheat the oven to 180°C (th. 6).

Roll out two-thirds of the pastry, then line a tart ring of about 22 cm in diameter. Spread the raspberry jam over the base. Use the remaining third of the pastry to cut strips and arrange them in a lattice pattern over the top of the tart.

Bake for about 45 minutes.

Rhubarb, Gin and Verbena Baba

Serves 6

For the baba dough
30 g butter
60 ml milk
80 g eggs (2 small eggs)
140 g flour
15 g caster sugar
3 g salt
6 g baker's yeast
Zest of ½ unwaxed lemon

For the soaking syrup
150 g caster sugar
40 ml lemon juice
4 g dried verbena
200 ml gin

For the rhubarb marmalade
400 g rhubarb
1 vanilla pod
60 g glucose
24 g caster sugar
8 g pectin NH nappage
2 gelatine leaves

For the gin crème fraîche
150 g crème fraîche
50 ml double cream
20 ml gin

Melt the butter. Using the paddle attachment of a mixer, combine all the other ingredients. Add the melted, lukewarm butter.

Once the mixture is homogeneous, pipe 25 g into each mould (Silikomart® sphere moulds). Leave to prove in a warm place for about 1 hour, until the mixture reaches the top of the mould.

Preheat the oven to 165°C (th. 5/6), then bake for 25 minutes. Unmould the babas as soon as they come out of the oven and leave to cool.

In a saucepan, bring 400 ml of water to the boil with the sugar, lemon juice and verbena. Remove from the heat, cover and leave the verbena to infuse for 30 minutes, then strain. Add the gin. Soak the babas in the hot syrup until they are thoroughly saturated.

Peel the rhubarb stalks and cut them into large cubes. In a saucepan, cook them gently with the seeds scraped from the split vanilla pod and the glucose. Add the sugar and pectin mixture in a thin sprinkling, bring to the boil for 5 minutes, then incorporate the gelatine leaf previously softened in cold water. Mix well, then chill the marmalade for 1 hour.

Mix the two creams and the gin together in a bowl.

In a deep plate, spoon a layer of rhubarb marmalade, place a baba on top, and serve with the gin crème fraîche.

Photo of the recipe on the next page

DESSERTS

Light Chestnut Mousse

Serves 4

For the blown sugar
100 g isomalt
1 drop brown colouring

For the hazelnut sablé
25 g butter
12 g icing sugar
15 g hazelnut powder
30 g T45 flour

For the mandarin sorbet
22 g water
22 g sugar
1 g stabiliser
2 g mandarin zest
130 g mandarin juice
8 g lemon juice

For the chestnut emulsion
200 g milk
200 g cream
60 g egg yolks
10 g sugar
50 g chestnut purée

For the tuile
80 g chestnut purée

Melt the isomalt gradually with the drop of colouring, then allow it to cool. Blow sugar bubbles using a sugar pump. Hollow them out on a hot ring. Set aside.

Prepare the hazelnut sablé by mixing the butter, icing sugar, hazelnut powder and flour. Spread the mixture on a baking tray. It should be a few millimetres thick. Bake at 170°C (th.5/6) for 15 minutes. Then cut out 4 cm discs from the baked dough.

Make the mandarin sorbet: bring the water, sugar, stabiliser and mandarin zest to the boil. Remove from the heat, pour in the mandarin and lemon juices, then churn in an ice-cream maker.

Prepare the chestnut emulsion. Bring the milk and cream to the boil. Whisk the egg yolks and sugar until pale, then pour the boiling liquid over them and cook as an anglaise at 85 °C. Add the chestnut purée and blend. Once cooled, pour into a siphon and charge with two cartridges.

Prepare the tuile. Using a stencil shaped like a horse-chestnut leaf, spread the chestnut purée onto a silicone mat. Bake at 170°C (th.5/6) until lightly coloured. Unmould and allow to cool.

To plate, place a ball of mandarin sorbet on the hazelnut sablé, surround the sorbet with the chestnut emulsion, then add the blown sugar decoration and the chestnut-leaf tuile.

Photo of the recipe on the next page

Opposite: Barbara Koch.

Apple Cake Tatin-Style

For 6 individual cakes

For the apple cake
15 cooking apples
100 g caster sugar (1)
150 g caster sugar (2)
20 g pectin NH nappage

For the hazelnut sablé
150 g softened butter
70 g icing sugar
165 g flour
80 g hazelnut powder

Make a dry caramel with the sugar (1), then pour the caramel into a rectangular tin of about 20 × 10 cm previously lined with baking paper.

Preheat the oven to 175 °C (th. 5/6). Peel, core, and slice the apples very thinly using a mandoline. Arrange the slices in the tin, sprinkling between each layer with the mixture of sugar (2) and pectin. Cover with aluminium foil and bake for 1 hour to 1 hour and 30 minutes, keeping an eye on the cooking; the apples should be well coloured without burning. Leave to cool in the fridge, turn out, then cut with a pastry cutter into the desired shape.

Preheat the oven to 165 °C (th. 5/6). In a mixer, blend the softened butter with the icing sugar without incorporating air. Add the flour and the hazelnut powder, mixing until you obtain a smooth dough. Roll out to about 3 mm thick on a baking tray lined with baking parchment or a silicone mat. Bake for about 8 minutes, cut according to the shape of the apple cakes and finish baking until lightly golden brown.

Arrange the apple cake and serve warm, accompanied by a scoop of vanilla ice cream or a spoonful of thick double cream.

Kougelhopf

Serves 8

500 g flour
15 g baker's yeast
125 ml milk
10 g salt
125 g caster sugar
3 eggs
250 g soft unsalted butter extra for the mould
100 g Malaga raisins
100 ml kirsch
A few whole almonds
Icing sugar for dusting

Prepare the starter: dissolve the yeast in the lukewarm milk.

Add around 200 g of the flour to make a firm dough.

Leave to rise in a warm place.

Soak the Malaga raisins in a little kirsch.

Place the remaining flour in a mixing bowl. Add the salt, sugar and the rest of the lukewarm milk. Mix, then incorporate the eggs and half of the softened butter. Beat the dough well and gradually add the remaining butter. Aerate the dough thoroughly by lifting and stretching it.

Finally, incorporate the starter, which should have doubled in volume. Beat for a few more minutes. The dough should come away from the sides of the bowl.

Add the drained Malaga raisins at this stage.

Cover with a clean cloth and leave to rise in a warm place for 1 hour and 30 minutes.

When the dough has doubled in volume, knock it back with your hands.

Butter the kougelhopf mould and place a whole almond in each groove.

Add the dough. Leave to prove again in a warm place until it reaches the rim of the mould, about 45 minutes.

Preheat the oven to 180 °C (th. 6), then bake for 1 hour.

Remove the kougelhopf from the mould, leave to cool and dust with icing sugar.

"Kougelhopf, a culinary symbol of Alsace, every Alsatian family has its own recipe."

Opposite: Marc and his daughter Laetitia.

DESSERTS 227

Chocolate Cookie

Serves 4 to 6

For the cookie dough
125 g dark chocolate
125 g pecan nuts
185 g softened butter
300 g light brown sugar
95 g eggs (2 small eggs)
280 g flour
6 g baking powder
2 g bicarbonate of soda
6 g fleur de sel

For the moelleux mixture
230 g dark chocolate
230 g butter
290 g caster sugar
370 g eggs (6 eggs)
100 g flour

Toast the pecan nuts and chop them roughly; chop the chocolate as well. In the bowl of a mixer fitted with the paddle attachment, combine the softened butter with the brown sugar, then add the eggs, the dry ingredients and the fleur de sel. Finish by incorporating the pecan nuts and the chocolate.

Spread the mixture between two sheets of baking parchment to a thickness of about 1 cm and chill until firm.

Melt the chocolate and the butter. Whisk together the sugar and the eggs without incorporating air, then add the melted butter and chocolate mixture. Finish by folding in the sifted flour.

In a frying pan 10 or 15 cm in diameter that is ovenproof, spread about 2 cm of the moelleux mixture, place on top a disc of the cookie dough, and bake in the oven at 190°C (th. 7) for about 10 minutes. The outside should be crisp, and the inside still molten. Chocolate shards may be added on top of the cookie after baking.

Peach Haeberlin

Originally named by my father "peach à l'impératrice", in homage to my grandmother who worshipped Napoleon Bonaparte

Serves 6

6 peaches poached in vanilla syrup

For the pistachio ice cream
500 ml milk
500 ml whipping cream
250 g caster sugar
5 egg yolks
100 g pistachio paste

For the Champagne sabayon
1 bottle of Champagne
16 egg yolks
300 g caster sugar
Whipped cream (Chantilly) for decoration

Prepare the ice cream. In a saucepan, bring the milk and cream to the boil with half of the sugar.

In a mixing bowl, whisk the egg yolks with the remaining sugar, then pour the boiling liquid over them while whisking continuously. Return the mixture to a low heat (or a bain-marie) and cook until it coats the back of a spoon, about 10 minutes, stirring constantly with a wooden spoon.

Remove from the heat, add the pistachio paste, pass through a fine sieve and churn in an ice-cream maker.

Prepare the sabayon. In a saucepan, whisk the egg yolks with the sugar until the mixture lightens. Add the bottle of Champagne. Set over a bain-marie on low heat and whisk until the mixture thickens. Remove from the heat and continue whisking until cooled. Refrigerate.

To serve each portion: on a large deep plate, place one peach together with a scoop of pistachio ice cream. Spoon over the Champagne sabayon and decorate with a little whipped cream.

Rhubarb Meringue Tart

Serves 6 to 8

For the sweet pastry
300 g softened butter
190 g icing sugar
60 g ground almonds
2 eggs
1 pinch of salt
1 vanilla pod
500 g flour

For the rhubarb cubes
1 kg rhubarb
150 g caster sugar

For the custard filling
300 ml whipping cream
2 eggs
50 g caster sugar
5 g cornflour

For the meringue
200 g egg whites
200 g caster sugar
200 g icing sugar

Peel the rhubarb stalks, cut them into large cubes, then mix them with the sugar and leave them to macerate — allowing the rhubarb to release its juices — for at least 2 hours. Drain the cubes to remove the liquid.

Mix together the butter, icing sugar and ground almonds. Add the eggs, the salt, the seeds scraped from the split vanilla pod, then the flour, and mix gently. Form into a ball, wrap, and chill in the refrigerator for at least 1 hour.

Blend together the ingredients for the custard filling.

Prepare the meringue. Using a mixer, whip the egg whites while gradually incorporating the caster sugar, then fold in the sifted icing sugar using a spatula.

Preheat the oven to 180°C (th. 6). Roll out the sweet pastry thinly, line a tart ring of about 22 cm in diameter, add the rhubarb cubes and bake for about 15 minutes. Pour over the custard mixture, then return to the oven for a further 30 minutes. Pipe the meringue using a large star nozzle and place briefly in the oven at 220°C (th. 8/9) for about 3 minutes.

DESSERTS 237

Above: Pascal Hainigue, pastry chef, in the middle of his team, in the foreground: Hugo Loisel, pastry sous-chef.

Ghana Chocolate Dessert in Textures

Serves 4

For the gavotte
240 g water
2 g salt
20 g butter
55 g icing sugar
20 g T45 flour
8 g cocoa powder
2 small egg whites

For the chocolate crémeux
65 g milk
65 g cream
1 large egg yolk
6 g light brown sugar
24 g Nyangbo chocolate (68% cocoa)
24 g cocoa paste

For the almond and nib praline
17 g caster sugar
4 g water
36 g whole almonds
17 g cocoa nibs
6 g grapeseed oil

For the crisp layer
25 g Caraïbe chocolate (66% cocoa)
24 g grapeseed oil
60 g crêpes dentelles
13 g cocoa nibs

For the mucilage sorbet
200 g water
4 g ice-cream stabiliser
27 g atomised glucose
40 g sugar
85 g mucilage

For the gavotte

Preheat the oven to 170°C (th.6). Bring the water, salt and butter to the boil.

In a mixing bowl, sift together the icing sugar, flour and cocoa, then add the egg whites. Pour the boiling liquid onto the whites in two additions and mix. Spread the mixture on a baking tray to a thickness of 1 mm.

Spread evenly and bake at 170°C (th.6) for 25 minutes.

Turn the gavotte out onto baking parchment.

Leave overnight in a cool place to absorb moisture.

Cut into 10 cm discs with a cutter.

Place each gavotte on the centre of a lightly greased small tart mould, and place another mould on top to shape it.

Bake for 7 minutes at 160°C (th.5). Unmould while hot and store in a dry place.

For the chocolate crémeux

Bring the milk and cream to the boil, pour over the yolk mixed with the light brown sugar, then pour directly onto the mixture of melted chocolate and cocoa paste. Blend and allow to cool.

For the almond and nib praline

Make a dry caramel with the sugar: add the sugar and water little by little to a saucepan over low heat, stirring until a caramel forms.

Pour onto a silicone mat or paper-lined tray.

Roast the whole almonds in the oven until light brown inside.

Once cooled, blend the caramel into a powder.

Blend the almonds and cocoa nibs; add the grapeseed oil and finish mixing with the paddle attachment of a mixer.

For the crisp layer

Mix the melted chocolate with the grapeseed oil, then add the crêpes dentelles and the cocoa nibs.

For the mucilage sorbet

Heat the water to 40°C, add the stabiliser, atomised glucose and sugar, then bring to the boil. Pour over the mucilage pulp.

Leave to mature overnight in the refrigerator and churn in an ice-cream maker.

For the chocolate siphon emulsion
210 g milk
72 g cream
2 large egg yolks
15 g sugar
50 g chocolate

For the chocolate siphon emulsion

Make an anglaise cooked to 85°C with the milk, cream, yolks and sugar.

Pour the hot anglaise over the chocolate and blend.

Allow to cool. Charge in a siphon with two cartridges.

For plating

Place a gavotte on the plate, pipe the chocolate crémeux onto it.

Add the praline on top of the crémeux and a little crispy mixture.

Place a spoonful of mucilage sorbet in the centre, then use the siphon to form a dome of emulsion over the preparation.

Dust with a little vanilla powder (made by blending vanilla pod husks) and some cocoa nibs.

DESSERTS

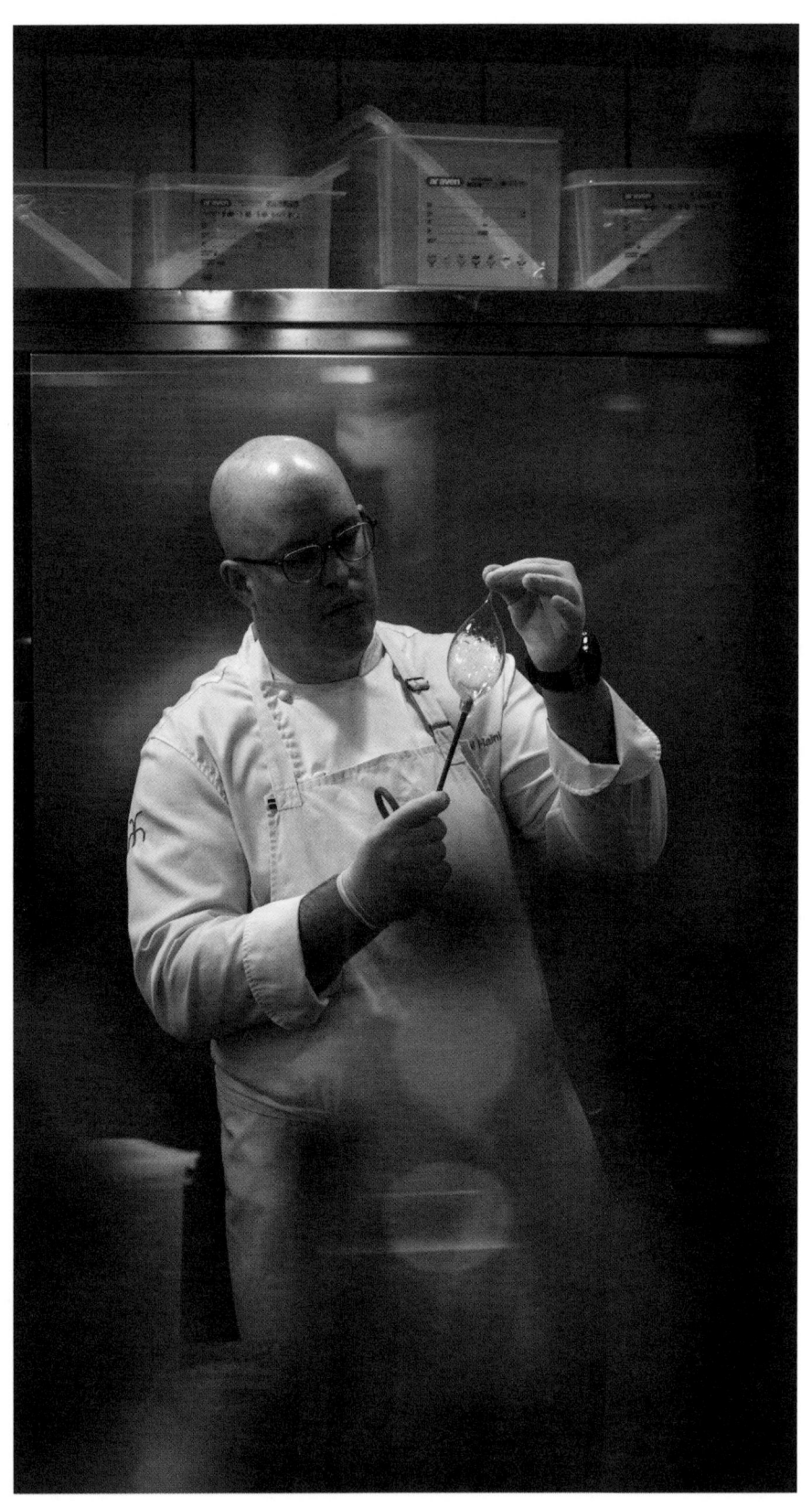

The Coffee Drop

Serves 4

For the coffee crème brûlée
160 g cream
26 g coffee beans
20 g light brown sugar
2 small egg yolks
10 g butter

For the coffee emulsion
180 g milk
180 g cream
80 g coffee beans
4 egg yolks
60 g sugar
1 gelatine leaf

For the hazelnut sablé
65 g butter
30 g icing sugar
70 g flour
35 g hazelnut powder

For the isomalt drop
200 g isomalt

For the coffee and orange blossom ice cream
65 g coffee beans
260 g milk
80 g light brown sugar
1 egg yolk
25 g butter
24 g orange blossom water

For the coffee crème brûlée

Bring the cream to the boil, add the coarsely crushed coffee beans and leave to infuse for 30 minutes. Strain through a fine sieve and top back up to the initial weight with cream. Reheat the cream to 40°C and add the light brown sugar. Bring to the boil for 1 minute, then pour over the egg yolks, add the butter, blend, then pour into a flexible mould (such as Flexipan®) to a height of 1.5 cm and freeze.

For the coffee emulsion

Bring the milk and cream to the boil, add the coarsely crushed coffee beans and leave to infuse for 30 minutes. Strain through a fine sieve and top back up to the initial weight with milk. Make a custard: bring the milk and cream back to the boil, whisk the egg yolks with the sugar until pale, pour over some of the hot milk while whisking, return the mixture to the saucepan and cook gently, stirring continuously. Once the custard has thickened, incorporate the gelatine, allow to cool, transfer to a siphon and charge with two cartridges.

For the hazelnut sablé

In a mixer, combine the softened butter with the icing sugar without incorporating air. Add the flour and hazelnut powder and mix until a homogeneous dough forms. Roll out between two sheets of baking paper to a thickness of 1 cm. Bake on a silicone mat (Silpat® type) at 165°C (th.5) for about 8 minutes. Place another sheet of baking paper on top and roll again, then cut out 42-mm discs and return to the oven for a further 2–3 minutes.

For the isomalt drop

Melt the isomalt gradually, allow to cool slightly. Blow sugar drops using a blowing bulb. Hollow them out on a heated ring.

For the coffee and orange blossom ice cream

Pour the crushed coffee beans into the boiling milk and leave to infuse for 30 minutes. Strain through a fine sieve and top back up to the initial weight with milk. Heat the milk and add the dry ingredients once it reaches 40°C. Cook as a custard and strain over the butter, add the orange blossom water, and blend.

For the plating

Cut the frozen crème brûlée using a 4-cm diameter cutter. Stack 3 sablé discs and 2 crème brûlée discs, alternating the layers. Place a scoop of ice cream on the discs. Take the isomalt drop by the tip, turn it over and fill it with the emulsion. Very delicately, using a small spoon, spread the emulsion over the sides of the drop, then place the filled drop on top of the stacked discs and ice-cream scoop. Dust lightly with vanilla powder.

Appendices

RECIPE TABLE

Starters

Haeberlin Foie Gras Terrine – p.17
Winter Lamb's Lettuce Salad with Roasted Beetroot and Alsace Horseradish Cream – p.19
Trout Fillet au Bleu on Ostergruss Radish with Lovage – p.22
Warm Goose Foie Gras with Apples and Truffle Sauce – p.25
Pâté de campagne with four meats, as Paul Haeberlin Loved It – p.26
Alsatian Onion Tarte Tatin – p.28
Blue Lobster Salad with Green Mango – p.31
Asparagus Feuilleté with Fresh Morels in Vin Jaune– p.33
Illhaeusern-Style Fried Carp with Japanese Mayonnaise – p.36
"Auberge de l'Ill" Sardine Tin with Oscietra Caviar– p.39

Soups

Detox Vegetable Broth – p.45
Chicken Consomme with Matzo-Meal Quenelles – p.46
Leek and Potato Velouté with White Truffle from Piedmont – p.53
Watercress Velouté with Poached Egg – p.57
Crayfish Broth with Aromatics – p.60

Side Dishes & Vegetables

Carrots in Kadaïf – p.74
Ceps from the Vosges Roasted in Fig Leaves– p.77
Little Cabbage Parcels Stuffed with Truffle– p.81
Spelt Risotto with Ceps – p.82
Green Bean Salad with Poached Egg and Foie Gras – p.85
Wood-Roasted Aubergines with Natural Vinaigrette – p.86
Ratte Potatoes Cooked in Hay – p.88
Red Cabbage Confit with Figs – p.91

Fish

Mackerel in White Wine with Japanese-Style Daikon – p.95
Frog Mousseline Paul Haeberlin – p.96
Matelote of Illhaeusern with Riesling – p.98
Roast Eel in Hay – p.102
Zander Fillet à la Tante Henriette– p.107
Auberge de l'Ill Salmon Soufflé – p.110
Shellfish Broth with Seaweed and Scallops – p.113
Sole with Crayfish – p.114
Poached Thick-Cut Turbot with Hollandaise Sauce and Potatoes– p.117
Ragout of Lobster and Calf's Head with Pearl Barley– p.118

Meats

Beef Blade in Pinot Noir with Stuffed Marrow Bone – p.130
Whole Roasted Veal Kidneys in Fat with Madeira Sauce and Timut Pepper – p.134
Alsatian Spätzle – p.137
Veal Sweetbreads – p.140
Pig's Trotter Stuffed with Truffle – p.142
Pigeon Tournedos with Cabbage and Truffle – p.146
Miéral Bresse Chicken Poached Demi-Deuil – p.149
Viennese Escalope as My Grandmother Used to Make It – p.151
Traditional Stuffed Duckling – p.153
Veal Shank Marrakech-Inspired – p.156
Brasserie des Haras Choucroute Garnie – p.160
Herb-Roasted Rack of Lamb – p.163
Potatoes Cooked Munster-Valley Style with Black Olives and Thyme – p.164

Game

Spice-Lacquered Mallard – p.175
Roast Pheasant on Sauerkraut – p.179
Venison Medallions with Chartreuse Sauce – p.181
Partridge Romanov – p.187
Lièvre à la Royale – p.189
Woodcock Pie (Club des 100) – p.196

Desserts

Roasted Figs with Fig-Leaf Ice Cream – p.202
Vanilla and Raspberry Iced Vacherin, as My Grandmother Marthe Made It – p.205
Cherry Crêpes – p.209
Linzer Tart – p.210
Rhubarb, Gin and Verbena Baba – p.215
Light Chestnut Mousse – p.219
Apple Cake Tatin-Style – p.223
Kougelhopf – p.224
Chocolate Cookie – p.231
Peach Haeberlin – p.233
Rhubarb Meringue Tart – p.236
Ghana Chocolate Dessert in Textures – p.240
The Coffee Drop – p.244

RECIPE INDEX

Auberge de l'Ill Sardine Tin with Oscietra Caviar – p.39
Alsatian Onion Tarte Tatin – p.28
Alsatian Spätzle – p.137
Apple Cake Tatin-Style – p.223
Asparagus Feuilleté with Fresh Morels in Vin Jaune – p.33
Auberge de l'Ill Salmon Soufflé – p.110

Beef Blade in Pinot Noir with Stuffed Marrow Bone – p.130
Blue Lobster Salad with Green Mango – p.31
Brasserie des Haras Choucroute Garnie – p.160

Carrots in Kadaïf – p.74
Ceps from the Vosges Roasted in Fig Leaves – p.77
Cherry Crêpes – p.209
Chicken Consomme with Matzo-Meal Quenelles – p.46
Chocolate Cookie – p.231
Crayfish Broth with Aromatics – p.60

Detox Vegetable Broth – p.45

Frog Mousseline Paul Haeberlin – p.96

Ghana Chocolate Dessert in Textures – p.240
Green Bean Salad with Poached Egg and Foie Gras – p.85

Haeberlin Foie Gras Terrine – p.17
Herb-Roasted Rack of Lamb – p.163

Illhaeusern-Style Fried Carp with Japanese Mayonnaise – p.36

Kougelhopf – p.224

Leek and Potato Velouté with White Truffle from Piedmont – p.53
Lièvre à la Royale – p.189
Light Chestnut Mousse – p.219
Linzer Tart – p.210
Little Cabbage Parcels Stuffed with Truffle – p.81

Mackerel in White Wine with Japanese-Style Daikon – p.95
Matelote of Illhaeusern with Riesling – p.98
Miéral Bresse Chicken Poached Demi-Deuil – p.149

Partridge Romanov – p.187
Pâté de campagne with four meats, as Paul Haeberlin Loved It – p.26

Peach Haeberlin – p.233
Pig's Trotter Stuffed with Truffle – p.142
Pigeon Tournedos with Cabbage and Truffle – p.146
Poached Thick-Cut Turbot with Hollandaise Sauce and Potatoes – p.117
Potatoes Cooked Munster-Valley Style with Black Olives and Thyme – p.164

Ragout of Lobster and Calf's Head with Pearl Barley – p.118
Ratte Potatoes Cooked in Hay – p.88
Red Cabbage Confit with Figs – p.91
Rhubarb Meringue Tart – p.236
Rhubarb, Gin and Verbena Baba – p.215
Roast Eel in Hay – p.102
Roast Pheasant on Sauerkraut – p.179
Roasted Figs with Fig-Leaf Ice Cream – p.202

Shellfish Broth with Seaweed and Scallops – p.113
Sole with Crayfish – p.114
Spelt Risotto with Ceps – p.82
Spice-Lacquered Mallard – p.175

The Coffee Drop – p.244
Traditional Stuffed Duckling – p.153
Trout Fillet au Bleu on Ostergruss Radish with Lovage – p.22

Vanilla and Raspberry Iced Vacherin, as My Grandmother Marthe Made It – p.205
Veal Shank Marrakech-Inspired – p.156
Veal Sweetbreads – p.140
Venison Medallions with Chartreuse Sauce – p.181
Viennese Escalope as My Grandmother Used to Make It – p.151

Warm Goose Foie Gras with Apples and Truffle Sauce – p.25
Watercress Velouté with Poached Egg – p.57
Whole Roasted Veal Kidneys in Fat with Madeira Sauce and Timut Pepper – p.134
Winter Lamb's Lettuce Salad with Roasted Beetroot and Alsace Horseradish Cream – p.19
Woodcock Pie (Club des 100) – p.196
Wood-Roasted Aubergines with Natural Vinaigrette – p.86

Zander Fillet à la Tante Henriette – p.107

ADDRESSES

IN ALSACE

L'Auberge de l'Ill
2, rue de Collonges au Mont d'Or
68970 Illhaeusern
www.auberge-de-l-ill.com

Les Haras
23, rue des Glacières
67000 Strasbourg
www.les-haras-brasserie.com

IN JAPAN

L'Auberge de l'Ill Tokyo
1-6-4 Nishi-Azabu, Minato-ku, Tokyo
106-0031

L'Auberge de l'Ill Nagoya
42F Midland Square 4-7-1 Meieki,
Nakamura-ku, Nagoya-shi, Aichi

L'Auberge de l'Ill Saporo
3-1, S1 W28 Chuo-ku, Sapporo-shi,
Hokkaido

EPICES ASSOCIATION

EPICES Kennedy
44, avenue du Président Kennedy
68200 Mulhouse

EPICES Fonderie
16, rue de la Fonderie
68100 Mulhouse
www.epices.asso.fr

ACKNOWLEDGEMENTS

Marc Haeberlin
To my family,
To my teams,
To our guests.

To Laure, Agathe, Garlone, Laurence, Caroline, Laurent, Paul-Henry, for watching over this book.

Laurent Dupont would like to sincerely thank Marc and Isabelle Haeberlin for their great kindness and constant generosity; the entire team at the Auberge de l'Ill for their availability; Laure Aline and Agathe Masson (La Martinière) for their trust and for this wonderful human adventure; Garlone Bardel for those intense yet immensely rewarding days; and Laurence Maillet for taking such great care of my images.

Garlone Bardel
Thanks to Agnès Kobarta – Adèle Collections, who brought colour, texture, and a delicate yet profound soul to the compositions – pages 16, 29, 97, 99, 103, 116, 143, 147.
Thanks to the invaluable work of the ceramic artists, which makes each photograph so distinctive.
Brutal Céramique (Benoît Audureau, Potry …) – pages 23, 34, 37, 75, 84, 87, 90, 99, 111, 112, 115, 116, 131, 141, 147, 216.
Yu Uchida, wooden plates – pages 16, 44, 94, 103, 204.
Marion Graux – pages 80, 89.
Manon Clouzeau – pages 52, 97, 155.
Jérôme Hirson – page 29.
Rina Menardi – pages 106, 150, 157, 179, 186.
Joe Christopherson – page 61.

Published in 2026 by
Grub Street
4 Rainham Close
London
SW11 6SS

Email: food@grubstreet.co.uk
Web: www.grubstreet.co.uk
Twitter: @grub_street
Facebook: Grub Street Publishing
Instagram: grubstreet_books

Copyright this English language edition © Grub Street 2025
ISBN 978-1-911714-34-7
A CIP catalogue for this book is available from the British Library

Published originally in French as *L'Auberge De L'Ill au fil de l'eau*
© 2024 Éditions de La Martinière, an imprint of EDLM
Editorial Director: Laure Aline
Editor: Agathe Masson
Assistant Editor: Marine Laurençot
Production Manager: Titouan Roland
Design and Graphic Production: Laurence Maillet

All rights reserved. No part of this publication may be reproduced, stored in a retrieval system or transmitted in any form or by any means electronic, mechanical, photocopying, recording or otherwise without the prior permission of the publisher.

Printed and bound by Finidr